ROYAL SCOTS IN THE GULF

ROYAL SCOTS IN THE GULF

1st Battalion, The Royal Scots,
(The Royal Regiment)
on Operation GRANBY 1990–1991

by

LAURIE MILNER

with a Foreword by

General Sir Peter de la Billière
KCB KBE DSO MC

LEO COOPER
LONDON

First published in Great Britain in 1994 by
LEO COOPER
190 Shaftesbury Avenue, London, WC2H 8JL

an imprint of
Pen & Sword Books Ltd
47 Church Street, Barnsley, South Yorkshire, S70 2AS

Copyright © 1994 by Laurie Milner
ISBN 0 85052 273 0

A CIP catalogue record for this book is available
from the British Library

Typeset in Garamond by
CentraCet Limited, Cambridge
Printed By
Redwood Books
Trowbridge, Wilts.

CONTENTS

Contents

FOREWORD

by General Sir Peter de la Billière
KCB KBE DSO MC

After every conflict there follows an attempt to put it into historical perspective and to provide an historical record. We have had the photographic essays, and the journalists' accounts of the Gulf War. We have also had personal accounts written by senior commanders, my own included.

Now here is a history of The Royal Scots, one of the units which took part in the ground war. But this is not just a military history, it is the story of the individuals who make up a fighting battalion of infantry. From the Commanding Officer, an experienced soldier who stamped his personality on every aspect of the battalion's work, through the Company Commanders and their young Platoon Commanders, some not long out of Sandhurst, to the private soldiers, some of whom were decorated for assuming responsibility way beyond their age, rank and experience.

In the preface to my own account I wrote: '*My primary aim in writing this book is to demonstrate the importance of individual human beings in modern warfare. In the battle to drive the Iraqi army out of Kuwait, Coalition forces used*

*every form of high-technology weapon available; yet in the
end success depended on the performance of individuals,
whether they were pilots, divers, tank drivers, mechanics,
engineers, cooks, radio operators, infantrymen, nurses or
officers of all ranks. It was these ordinary people who, at the
end of the day were going to put their lives on the line and
risk their necks when their Government decided to go to
war.'*

This is the story of some of the individuals I was proud
to have under my command.

ACKNOWLEDGEMENTS

I owe a great debt of thanks to Iain Johnstone for his support and hospitality especially in the early stages of my research, and to his successor Bill Sylvester for allowing me to visit the Battalion during a busy period when they were training for a tour in South Armagh. In addition to the Royal Scots with whom I recorded interviews, I would like to thank Alex Alderson, Andrew Burnett, Rob Dickson, David Jack, George Lowder, Andy MacDowall, Mick Low, Tony Restall, Norman Soutar, Steve Telfer, Charlie Wallace and Mike Onslow for their help, hospitality and friendship during my visits to Werl and Inverness and during my subsequent research.

I would like to thank my colleagues at the Imperial War Museum: Peter Simkins, Mark Seaman, Neil Young, Catherine Moriarty, Terry Charman, Margaret Brooks, Ron Brooker, Derek Needham, Peter Cracknell, Dave Curtis and Brad King, for their help and tolerance. I would like to thank John Harding of the Army Historical Branch for his support and advice, and Nicholas Benson, author of

Acknowledgements

Rat's Tales, the history of the Staffordshire Regiment in the Gulf.

On the publishing side, thanks are due to Sir Nicholas Hewitt, Leo Cooper and Tom Hartman for providing the wherewithal to produce this book, and to Toby Buchan and John Bayne for their support, especially in the early stages of this project. Thanks also to Mike Moore, formerly of *Today*, now with the *Daily Mirror*, for permission to use some of the photographs he took of the Royal Scots when he accompanied them into action.

Last but not least, I would like to thank my wife Sue for her forbearance.

INTRODUCTION

When writing history within living memory it is essential not only to strive for objectivity but also to satisfy the participants, many of whom inevitably have a partial and therefore subjective view of events.

Because the official papers relating to this conflict are subject to the Official Secrets Act and are therefore closed for at least 30 years, it has been necessary to rely on the official despatch published in the *London Gazette*, which is, not surprisingly, a very broad overview, supplemented by the recently published memoirs of Generals Schwarzkopf and de la Billière, and the recent historical appraisals published by HMSO, Greenhill Books, Arms and Armour Press and Faber and Faber.

But it is the summaries, prepared for internal use within the Battalion and for lectures, and the private diaries and recollections of the individual soldiers of all ranks who served with the Royal Scots in the Gulf which provide the flesh for my historical skeleton. Because I was able to meet and interview so many participants and record their eyewitness accounts, I have made extensive use of direct quotes from their reminiscences. These, I feel, give an insight into the unique atmosphere of a Scottish battalion at war which my words alone could not provide. But, of course, I take full responsibility for any errors of fact or interpretation, and it should be noted that the opinions expressed in this book are those of the individuals concerned and do not necessarily reflect Ministry of Defence policy.

At an early stage in my research for this book, Iain Johnstone, who commanded the Royal Scots in the Gulf, drew my attention to a remark made, during a post-war conference on Operation GRANBY, by General Rupert Smith, Commander of the British 1st Armoured Division: 'I am becoming less certain exactly when I knew what I now know.'

This is a very important point for every historian to bear in mind, especially when heavily reliant on soldiers' reminiscences. But it is also important for the reader to bear in mind that we all *now* know that the Iraqis will to fight was drastically diminished by the Coalition's air attacks and rocket artillery. However, for the men who took part in the ground war, going through 'the breach' into Iraq, and each objective they took, was very much a step into the unknown. For all they knew they could have met heavy resistance, with a formidable array of weapons and fire-power, at any time. Certainly they expected to take casualties, not least because of the Nuclear, Biological and Chemical (NBC) threat.

I hope then that this book is historically accurate, but also an acceptable record within the closely-knit ranks of the Royal Scots, and of course to a much wider readership.

Prologue

INTERVENING EAST OF SUEZ

"For the British . . . intervening East of Suez is like riding a bike: you never lose the knack."
John Sullivan, *Independent on Sunday*,
2 September, 1990

The history of the Middle East in the twentieth century is tangled and emotive and the on-going conflicts appear to have no solution. Although this is not the place for a detailed analysis of the history of the region, in the interest of providing a backdrop to the campaign described in this book, here follows a brief "thumbnail sketch" of the sequence of events which lead to the conflict in the Gulf in 1991.

It is perhaps appropriate that British forces should have played a major role in this conflict, for Britain has been inextricably entangled in the history of the Gulf region since before the First World War. Indeed there was almost an inevitability that Britain should become involved in ejecting the armed forces of Iraq (a state it had artificially created), from Kuwait (one of Britain's former protectorates). It could even be argued that the Gulf War of 1991 is part of the legacy of Britain's defeat of the Ottoman Empire in the First World War. For it was the politicians' and the senior military commanders' reluctance to give this "side show" the attention it demanded, or to give due consideration to the outcome of some of the decisions and promises that were made, which has resulted in almost continual conflict in the Middle East since 1918, although it has to be said that the emergence of a ruler such as Saddam Hussein, at any time, in any state, was likely to have led to conflict.

As long ago as 1899, Great Britain and Kuwait signed a treaty which ensured that Britain assumed control of Kuwaiti foreign affairs, thereby frustrating Germany's ambitions in the region. When, in 1914, Germany drew Turkey into the First World War, Britain declared Kuwait and Egypt to be protectorates. As well as providing forces to protect the Suez Canal, Britain sent an expeditionary force to the area then known as Mesopotamia to protect its interests in the, so far relatively unimportant, oil-fields of the vilayet[1] of Basra, which extended to the Persian Gulf. An ill-prepared advance on Baghdad by this force was followed by a siege and a humiliating defeat by the Turks, at Kut el Amara, in which an entire British Division was captured. But a second, more successful, British advance was subsequently mounted. Baghdad fell in March, 1917, and by the end of the war, after a last-minute dash to Mosul, Britain was in control of the whole of Mesopotamia.

During the war there had been some discussion about the fate of the former Ottoman Empire. A secret agreement signed in 1916 divided the region into spheres of influence, in direct conflict with promises made to the Arabs who had supported the Allied campaign against the Turks in the Hejaz.[2]

In April, 1920, Britain received a League of Nations Mandate after the conference at San Remo, to prepare the territory, now called Iraq, for independence. Partly due to an inability on the Civil Commissioner's part to formulate a clear policy for the area, and partly because three formerly separate vilayets had been arbitrarily united, a revolt against British rule broke out during the following summer.

In an effort to honour at least one of the promises made to the Arabs, on 27 August, 1921, the British Government installed Emir Faisal ibn Husain, a member of the Hashemite ruling family of the Hejaz, as King of the newly-created state of Iraq. The borders of Iraq were defined in 1922 by Sir Percy Cox.[3] In the presence of Ibn Saud, ruler of Saudi Arabia, he drew a line, in thick red pencil, from the head of the Gulf to the frontier with Trans Jordan (now Jordan), and then two more lines to create "neutral zones".

When Britain terminated the Mandate in 1932, Iraq became independent and was admitted to the League of Nations, but British influence continued. Two RAF bases were maintained at Habbaniya and Shaiba, and the military instructors to the Iraqi armed forces were British.

Emir Faisal died in 1933, and was succeeded by his son, Ghazi, whose rule ended prematurely when he was killed in a car crash in 1939. Ghazi was succeeded by his infant son Faisal II; Iraq was therefore ruled by the Prince Regent, Amir Abd Al Ilah, Faisal's uncle.

In 1940 the British government took a firm line with the Iraqi government because of its Prime Minister, Rashid Ali's connections with the Axis powers. General Wavell, the British Commander-in-Chief in the Middle East, proposed strong diplomatic action supported by financial and economic sanctions and a special envoy was sent to Baghdad to try to steady the situation. The War Cabinet approved these proposals and in November of that year an attempt was made to oust Rashid Ali from the Iraqi Cabinet. The Iraqis complained that the British had interfered in Iraqi internal affairs. However, in April, 1941, Rashid Ali led a revolt and deposed the Prince Regent. The now openly pro-Axis Iraqi Prime Minister sent his forces to besiege the British air base at Habbaniya. On 18 May "Habforce", a hastily assembled British relief column was despatched from Palestine into Iraq. Unsupported by their German allies, the Iraqi troops were soon defeated. The British column then advanced on Baghdad and restored the Prince Regent to power.

On 14 July, 1958, the Iraqi monarchy was overthrown in a popular coup by "Free Officers". The Republic of Iraq was established and King Faisal II, the Crown Prince, and the Prime Minister, Nuri as-Said, were all killed. The two principal architects of the coup were Brigadier (later General) Abdel Karim Qassem and Colonel (later Field Marshal) Abdel Salem Muhammad Aref. A power struggle ensued and Qassem emerged as the victor, with Aref under a sentence of death which was never carried out.

On 24 July, 1958, the Baath (Renaissance) Party founder, Michel Aflaq (a French-educated Christian Syrian), arrived in Baghdad and in October of the following year a Baathist hit team, which included a young student named Saddam Hussein, tried unsuccessfully to assassinate Qassem. Saddam was slightly wounded in the attempt and fled to Syria and then Egypt.

When, on 19 June, 1961, Kuwait's Independence was announced, Qassem claimed that Kuwait was part of Iraq and would not recognize the Independence agreement between Kuwait and Great Britain. This even prompted Saddam Hussein, still in exile in Egypt, to send Qassem, his former target for assassination, a telegram congratulating him. On 3 July, 1961, British Forces arrived in the Gulf once more, this time to defend Kuwait against a threatened Iraqi invasion.

On 8 February, 1963, Qassem was overthrown by a Baathist coup in the "Ramadam Revolution". Qassem's old adversary Abdel Salem Aref became President with Ahmed Hassan al-Bakr as Premier, and Saddam Hussein returned from exile. Aref, however, took direct control, with army backing, later that year and dismissed the Baathist ministers.

The Baath Party seized power in Iraq on 17 July, 1968, and a Revolutionary government was formed under Ahmed Hassan al-Bakr. By the end of the month it had been proclaimed that al-Bakr was to be Chairman of the Revolutionary Command Council, with Saddam Hussein as Deputy Chairman in charge of internal security.

During the next decade Iraq shifted its allegiance from West to East, and the seeds of the Iran-Iraq conflict, and ultimately the Gulf War, were sown. On 8 April, 1972, the Iraqi government signed a fifteen-year Treaty of Friendship and co-operation with the Soviet Union, and on 1 June nationalized its oil industry. Meanwhile President Nixon announced that the Shah of Iran could buy any non-nuclear weapons he wanted and promised American co-operation with Iran, (although this was to be short-lived and would cease in 1979 when the Shah was overthrown and the Ayatollah Khomeini came to power).

An Accord signed in Algiers, on 6 March, 1975, between Iran and Iraq gave Iran control of the Shatt al-Arab waterway in return for an end to Iranian support for Kurdish insurgents inside Iraq.

On 16 July, 1978, Saddam Hussein became President of Iraq, Chairman of the Revolutionary Command Council and Commander-in-Chief of the armed forces, and in October of the following year Iraq demanded revision of the Algiers agreement.

The war which followed between Iran and Iraq was to provide another link in the chain of events. As far as Iraq was concerned, it began on 4 September, 1980, when Iranian troops attacked two border towns on the Baghdad road. In retaliation, on 17 September Iraq abrogated the Algiers agreement, and on the 22nd Iraqi forces invaded Iran. The Iraqi advance was halted by unexpected resistance in appalling weather and the conflict soon degenerated into trench deadlock, reminiscent of the First World War on the Western Front, along the entire 750-mile frontier. Almost suicidal attacks by the Iranians eventually forced the Iraqis to announce their unilateral withdrawal from Iran on 30 June, 1982, but that was not end of the war. The Iranian forces pressed on and invaded northern Iraq. In March, 1984, came the first confirmed use of long-range missiles by the Iraqis against Iranian cities and in March of that year chemical weapons were used against the Kurds in the north, when some 5,000 inhabitants were killed in a poison-gas attack on Halabja.

But the Iranians could not sustain the offensive and were suffering heavy losses. Finally, on 18 July, 1988, Iran formally accepted the UN Security Resolution 598 which called for a cease-fire, and the war between Iran and Iraq ended.

Saddam Hussein proclaimed himself victor, but in fact both sides ended the war in much the same position as before the Iraqi invasion of September, 1980, albeit that both were considerably financially worse off. Although he has proved to be an unpredictable and even irrational leader, Saddam Hussein has tried to project the profile of the Saviour of the Arabs. His war against Iran, his invasion of Kuwait and his quest for nuclear weapons could all be seen as part of a plan to build up the military and financial might of Iraq so that he can attack Israel and perhaps ultimately challenge the international power of the United States. Saddam Hussein therefore needed a great victory to establish himself as the modern Arab saviour.

Until the overthrow of the Shah of Iran in 1979 and the apparent collapse of the Iranian Armed Forces, Iran was too powerful to challenge. With the coming to power of the Ayatollah Khomeini and his virulently anti-western, fundamentalist regime, Saddam Hussein probably calculated that he could rely on financial and material support from the

West and even from the United States, particularly as the new regime in Teheran had manifested itself in the seizure of the US Embassy and the taking hostage of its diplomatic staff in 1979.

Although it seems likely that his ultimate aim was to unite the Arab world and improve its international standing, it is ironic that in taking on Iran, Saddam Hussein lost the support of the Organization of Petroleum Exporting Countries (OPEC) because his action was thought to be undermining the unity of the oil cartel, just as it was emerging as a player in the international scene following the oil explosion in the early 1970s.

What Saddam Hussein craved most was power. The main source of power within the Middle East was the financial power afforded by oil, but Iraqi oil production did not match that of its neighbours, unless the disputed oilfields of Kuwait could be acquired. These could be acquired by force of arms, and it seems that fear of the spread of Islamic fundamentalism from Iran, together with a measure of blinkered economic opportunism, led many states to help provide Saddam Hussein with the ability to build the massive arsenal he needed.

As long as it remained a war of attrition, the Iran/Iraq conflict was safe. Indeed, it made good economic sense for almost anyone to support it. While it continued, the Iranians were being kept occupied and could not pursue an aggressive foreign policy towards other neighbouring states, and Iraq's arsenal was being steadily eroded while those supplying the arms and equipment were making money, not to mention providing employment.

Kuwait gave its neighbour, Iraq, massive financial support during the eight-year war with Iran, and the Kuwaiti government was surprised when it was asked to write off the debt. The Iraqis maintained that Kuwait had deliberately over-produced oil, bringing the price down, and, in July,

1990, further accused Kuwait of stealing $2.4 billion of Iraqi oil from the disputed wells.

On 2 August, 1990, Iraqi forces invaded Kuwait and, on the 28th, Iraq declared Kuwait to be its 19th province.

An oft repeated comment during the Gulf War was that "if Kuwait had produced carrots and not oil, the invasion would have been ignored by the west", but this is not entirely true. Saddam Hussein's military might was a monster created by many states, particularly those in the West which produce sophisticated weapons. It was ultimately a product of the capitalist ethos of free markets which allows any country to devote any amount of its gross national product to purchasing armaments. Sooner or later it would be necessary to reduce this might.

History is punctuated by "what ifs", and it is interesting to speculate on the outcome of the Gulf crisis if Saddam Hussein had occupied only the disputed oil-fields, or if, having invaded Kuwait, he had then sent his forces down the coast to take control of the Saudi Arabian ports thereby denying their use to the Coalition Forces.

Certainly, when his forces invaded Kuwait on 2 August, 1990, Saddam Hussein made a serious error in his timing. As far as the United Nations Security Council was concerned, for probably the first time any resolutions they passed could be backed up by military action, without the danger of an East/West confrontation and the possibility of escalation. As far as the British Armed Forces were concerned, Saddam sent his troops into Kuwait at the most opportune time, between the easing of East/West relations and the implementation of Options for Change. In short, it was probably the only time since the Second World War that the British Army could have sent an entire Armoured Division to the Middle East.

Iraq in the 1990s therefore remains an unhappy combination of three vilayets or provinces of the former Ottoman (Turkish) Empire: Basra – mainly populated by

Shiite Arabs; Baghdad – mainly populated by Sunni Arabs; and Mosul – mainly populated by Sunni Kurds, all united within borders created by the stroke of a pen wielded by Sir Percy Cox, the former British High Commissioner in Baghdad.

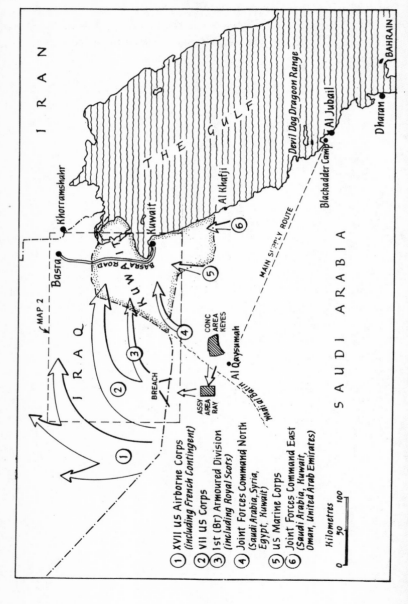

I R A N

Khorramshahr

THE GULF

Basra

← MAP 2

I R A Q

BASRA ROAD

Kuwait

Al Khafji

Devil Dog Dragoon Range

Al Jubail

Blackadder Camp

Dharan

BAHRAIN

BREACH

ASSY AREA RAY

Al Qaysumah

CONC AREA KEYES

Wadi al Batin

MAIN SUPPLY ROUTE

S A U D I   A R A B I A

① XVII US Airborne Corps
   (including French contingent)
② VII US Corps
③ 1st (Br) Armoured Division
   (including Royal Scots)
④ Joint Forces Command North
   (Saudi Arabia, Syria,
   Egypt, Kuwait)
⑤ US Marine Corps
⑥ Joint Forces Command East
   (Saudi Arabia, Kuwait,
   Oman, United Arab Emirates)

Kilometres

0   50   100

Chapter 1

A SECRET MESSAGE

"I have this secret message for you – because it's secret I can't tell you what it says!" This was my Field Officer of the Week ringing me up in Hammelberg, in Southern Germany.
Lt.Colonel Iain A. Johnstone OBE,
Commanding Officer

When news of the Iraqi invasion of Kuwait broke, 1st Battalion, The Royal Scots, (The Royal Regiment), to give it its full title at the time, was at Albuhera Barracks at Werl, near Dortmund. The "Royals" had been equipped with FV432 Armoured Personnel Carriers for about five years and had converted to "Warrior" Infantry Fighting Vehicles in 1989.

They were a formidable team under the command of Lieutenant Colonel Iain Johnstone. The son of a Battle of Britain fighter pilot, Iain Johnstone was, and is, a career officer with a distinguished record. Since his commission into the Regiment from Sandhurst in 1968, he has served in Northern Ireland, in Cyprus during the Turkish invasion in 1974, in Oman, where he commanded a Company of Arab soldiers during the Dhofar War, in Beirut where he was awarded the Order of the British Empire, and as a Company Commander in Germany. After garrison duty with the Royals in the Falklands in 1984, and another brief spell in Germany, he was attached to the Ministry of Defence. In

1986 he was sent to Beirut at short notice as Defence Attaché for eighteen months. Before taking command of the only remaining battalion of The Royal Scots in 1989, he was an instructor at the Army Staff College where he specialized in Armoured Warfare Tactics.

The Colonel was in my view a remarkable chap in so much as he had a strong belief in the Boyd Cycle[1], where you've got to get inside your opponent's decision-making cycle. If you can get inside it and make a decision before he has, he then starts changing his cycle. Once you get him to change what he is doing, particularly for instance if he is on the offensive, and he's changing what he's doing, well clearly you've unsettled him. The best way to achieve that is right down to the lowest level. The commanding officer's view is very much that: whilst he gave the parameters, the individual vehicle drivers, the individual soldiers almost, were free within those confines to do what they perceived to be the necessary way of achieving the mission.

Major Bryan C. Johnston, Commander, Fire Support Company

Iain Johnstone took command of the Royal Scots at the end of October, 1989, while they were undergoing their annual FTX (Field Training Exercise) at Soltau, only 40 kilometres from the East German border. Within a month of his arrival the Berlin Wall came down. This was to have great significance, not only in the west, but on the outcome of Saddam Hussein's ill-timed invasion of Kuwait. For the first time since the Second World War ended in 1945, the United States and Great Britain could release troops from Germany to fight elsewhere, and perhaps more significantly, because of the easing of the tension between East and West, for the first time they had the acquiescence, if not the actual support, of the Soviet Union.

Soon after Iain Johnstone's arrival the Royals returned to their home at Werl.

At the time of the Iraqi invasion the 3rd Division, of which the Battalion formed part, was about to be relegated to the role of Support Division, and the next significant date on the Royals' calendar was the "Arms Plot" move to Fort George, Inverness, in the spring of 1991. This would mark the end of six years with BAOR, an unusually long tour.

During July and August, 1990, the Battalion was on 50% leave and the few Jocks that were still around, in the camp and married quarters, seem to have paid little attention to the news of the invasion of Kuwait. Even among the officers, those who discussed it attached little importance to it and seem to have come to the conclusion that it would soon blow over.

I remember the very day, I was out in the play park with my kids and my wife was up on the balcony. My next door neighbour shouted from [his] balcony, "the Iraqis have invaded Kuwait!" I said, "What's that to me?"

Corporal Derek Notman, 6 Platoon, B Company

I remember the weekend quite well because I was down [doing] adventure training and I just remember it had been in the news, and meeting up with some of the other officers. They'd asked what had been happening in the previous week in the news because they hadn't seen a paper. So I just casually remarked that he'd invaded, and they all just sat there and said, "Oh", and that was that. I don't think any of us thought any more of it.

Lieutenant Wendy Smart, Second-in-Command,
Fire Support Company

The Commanding Officer, who had lived and worked in the Middle East, had a different opinion, however.

I think at that stage we thought there was a possibility that Iraq would continue on into Saudi Arabia and then fold up all the Gulf States because there isn't a lot of democracy in the Gulf. I think some of the rulers might be in a fairly perilous state if there was a popular uprising against them, which I think had Saudi Arabia begun to fold then, might have occurred. I think, the first perception was that we were going to go in, or the British Army was going to go in, as a holding, blocking operation, and might be involved in the destruction of an Iraqi attack. Certainly at that stage I don't think I harboured any ideas that we were actually going to attack [occupied] Kuwait.

Lt.Colonel Iain Johnstone

When BAOR requested an immediate appraisal of the manpower and vehicle states of the units under its command, the Royal Scots seemed to be an obvious choice to go, if British ground forces were to be sent to the Gulf. The Royals' high standard of training, as well as their levels of manpower and equipment, together with the fact that they were destined to leave Germany anyway, led most of the men to assume, understandably, but at this stage quite wrongly, that they would be chosen.

But early in September it seemed that not only would they not go to the Gulf but that they were to be used to guard the docks and to provide administrative support for 7th Armoured Brigade's departure.

We thought we were guaranteed to go; we were probably the only people that were nearly up to strength; we had the highest equipment availability and so we just assumed we would be sent for. So it was with disappointment that we heard that 7 Brigade were going and not us.

Lt.Colonel Iain Johnstone

The Battalion was being kept together, they weren't even taking gear off us. Everyone else was having vehicles taken off them, people taken off them, specialist bits of kit taken off them. The support weapons platoons were losing their TI [Thermal Imaging equipment] etc etc to bolster what there was among those that went. And we kept all ours, which was a very good sign that if anyone else was going to go then [the] chances were it would be us.

Lieutenant Colin Dougan, Commander, 8 Platoon, C Company

Apparently adding insult to injury, some of the Royals were detailed to assist in training some of the troops who were about to depart.

I had recently run the Divisional Indirect Fire Concentration at Hohne, which was where 3rd Division, which we belonged to, sent all of their artillery and all of their mortars to do all of their training. Whilst I was up there it was announced that the Staffords[2] would become the Battalion that was going to be going and so they were immediately tacked on to the Indirect Fire Concentration in preparation for their move off to Saudi.

Major Bryan Johnston

On 15 September the Warning Order came for the move to the docks to help 7 Brigade on its way. Battalion Headquarters and a reinforced C Company moved to Bremerhaven where the bulk of the Brigade's vehicles and equipment was to be embarked. This task was to last five weeks. B Company, meanwhile, moved to Emden to supervise the safe loading of the ammunition. This was to last a further fortnight.

My Company, I was in C Company at the time, rather than A Company, went off to Bremerhaven and we did the onerous task of Port Security, and a more dull job I don't think I'll ever be given! It seemed quite important and you're part of it all, but it was heartbreaking to see all these people, people I knew from Sandhurst, coming through and saying, "Hey, we're off!" They were all getting together, and there was me cutting around this dock, living in an ISO container, having my Jocks patrol round for these guys. They were going off to do it for real and we were sitting in a wet mouldy dock in Bremerhaven. B Company were in Emden doing the same thing with ammunition, we were doing the vehicles and people. They had an even worse task, they were doing it with ammunition and no faces, awful!

Lieutenant Colin Dougan

In the meantime the Battalion was still buzzing with rumours. A popular theory was that they would be sent out to reinforce 7 Brigade. After all, with the exception of some of the Mortar Platoon's kit, they had not been raided for equipment in the way that most of BAOR had. During September the Battalion was at last informed that it would be going to the Gulf, but not until April, 1991. Operation GRANBY 2 provided for a "roulement" tour – a replacement of men and equipment – so that the units deployed in Saudi Arabia could be relieved, presumably after the hostilities – if there were any – were over. Undaunted, the Battalion continued training. The Royals, who as an Armoured Infantry Battalion had won gunnery prizes, were sent for FIBUA (Fighting In Built Up Areas) training at Hammelberg as part of their build up for GRANBY 2. Although no strangers to this type of operation, having undertaken tours in Northern Ireland, some of the men were surprised that they should be deployed in anything other than their Armoured Infantry role, but concluded that perhaps this was preparation for a similar British presence in Kuwait City. It was while they were at Hammelberg that the Commanding Officer received the, now legendary, cryptic telephone message.

November 15th, we were rung up about midnight; the telephone conversation was rather strange in so much that it said "I have this secret message for you," and I said, "Yes?" and he said, "Because it's secret I can't tell you what it says!" So we had this fairly meaningless conversation to begin with and eventually it transpired that we were on G minus 14 and counting. In other words we had to be ready by the end of November. This was my Field Officer of the Week ringing me up in Hammelberg down in Southern Germany.

Lt.Colonel Iain Johnstone

I was Field Officer of the Week and the signal that came in was clearly a high classification so I drove into Camp with an extraordinary feeling of expectation. The Germans have got few speed restrictions on the roads but I must have got there in about two minutes flat! The Chief Clerk had got the signal in and he'd got a rough impression of what it might be, rang me and said, "Come and open it". Of course, by the time I got there, there was a team of about fifteen people waiting on the step, waiting for me to open this thing. The Battalion at that stage were down at Hammelberg and so I immediately ripped it open and it was the Warning Order.

The Colonel was in Hammelberg and I rang him with this sort of convoluted [message]. I had to chase him round Hammelberg anyway. Everywhere he went I left a message for him to ring me. I finally got through of course. He then made a move straight back up with the Battalion to start the planning.

Major Bryan Johnston

This then was the Warning Order for Operation GRANBY 1.5 which was to provide a further Armoured Brigade to complete the 1st (British) Armoured Division in Saudi Arabia.

The formal announcement was made in the House of Commons on 22 November, 1990, by the Rt Hon Tom King MP, Secretary of State for Defence. Bringing the British force up to a Division, under the command of Major-General Rupert Smith, enabled Lieutenant-General Sir Peter de la Billière, Commander of the British Forces in the Middle East, to petition for the increased British contingent to take a more central role in the plan of attack. Hitherto 7 Brigade had been providing additional armour for the US Marine Corps who were destined to create a diversion while the main offensive took place elsewhere.

The Royal Scots were to join the 4th Brigade which was being assembled under the command of Brigadier Christopher Hammerbeck. He sent a Training Directive to all the units in his new brigade reminding them of the urgency of their task and calling upon them to observe the maxim "Train Hard, Fight Easy". Commanders were reminded that it was essential that, while aiming for the very highest standards, they must ensure that each man fired the personal weapon he was taking to the Gulf, and also fired the weapons systems of the vehicle he was to crew in the Gulf.

There was no time to waste. With less than two weeks to get the Battalion ready for departure, Colonel Johnstone imposed a very strict régime on his men. This was echoed by his Company Commanders who did their utmost to ensure that the message went right through the chain of command so that the men were in no doubt at all that this would be the real thing.

As soon as we heard that a British contingent was going to be sent, I was in no doubt that we would go. We, as a battalion, would go to the Gulf and would fight a war. That was really drummed into me by somebody I used to work for at the Ministry of Defence, who was a Company Commander in the Falklands. His abiding words of wisdom [were] "If ever a conflict blows up somewhere in the world, and we're going to send troops there, always assume that you will go and always assume that you will fight. If you believe that and believe it one hundred percent you'll never be disappointed," and it was very hard initially to put that across to my men.

Major John Potter, Commander, B Company

Because they were going to the Gulf they were going to face a full-blooded enemy. It was none of this – where the terrorist pops up, shoots [at] you, then runs away whether or not one man gets hit and the rest of you are all right. We had to put over to the guys this is it. These people had the same as we had, could kill just as quickly and easily as we could kill. So we had to just instil it into the guys, it wasn't ten men against one man. We were facing a full force army and those guys were as determined to keep Kuwait as we were to take it. So that in itself made the guys realize that it's no BATUS, it's no Soltau, it's no Northern Ireland. They're going to war and they accepted that fact.

Sergeant Tom Gorrian, 5 Platoon, B Company

The new régime began with the closure of the Officers' and the Sergeants' Messes. All members of the Battalion were to take their meals in the cook-house, and in future married men would also eat with the rest of the Battalion, and only return to their quarters at the end of the day.

Each day began with fitness training for the whole Battalion and no excuses were tolerated; everyone had to take part.

You'd wake up at quarter to seven, go for a run at seven, work through the day till about nine, ten o'clock at night depending on what paperwork you had to have cracked and that was what you did. All those silly things that officers do, like your involvement in the Mess or whatever, were all removed, all the extraneous pressures on you were taken away. You weren't the officer who wandered back up to the Mess to enjoy your five-course dinner or whatever they thought you got up to. You became one of them and you worked harder than they did; you had to.

Lieutenant Alastair Stobie, Commander, 5 Platoon, B Company

Started at seven, Battalion fitness parade, every morning, which happened in the gym. The whole Battalion would be there and the Padre would have a quick five minutes or so, say the Regimental Collect. Ready, off we go for a run. It was amazing actually because the weather at that stage, we're really talking November, December here, was snow on the ground, there was snow on the ground! We'd go on these runs, down the hills at the back of the Stadt Wald, behind the camp, and we were running around with our gas-masks on. You run for fifteen minutes with your gas-mask on, freezing cold, only to be two months or a month later out in the desert, which was the exact opposite. So we were led to believe.

Lieutenant Guy S. Richardson, Commander, Anti-Tank Platoon

This sudden change brought with it a testing time for the Battalion as a whole, physically, mentally and spiritually. Although fighting a war is part of the soldier's job, some of the men had not expected to be called on to fight a full-scale war, and even the Padre had to prepare himself, as well as helping to prepare the Battalion, for the tremendous task ahead.

We had a couple of lads who found the whole war thing difficult, I suppose [some] people who, as they had served, had began to change their views about war or pacifism. It had never become an issue because they never thought they would be going to war. Suddenly when the reality that we were going to war came out, those things that were quietly mulling away inside had to be dealt with.

The Commanding Officer is a Christian man who was very aware of the need to look after the spiritual needs of the men and to give them some way of expressing spiritual feelings and communicating with God when the chips were down. So we began the pattern of starting early in the morning. I was unable to find out how long I had, but I kept [it] as short as I could and we gave everybody a New Testament and at the back there was a reading plan for a lesson for every day of the week. I would read the day's lesson and say a few words and say a prayer, and I felt very much that if I lost the men then, then I'd lost them. That if I couldn't find something relevant to say to them in that peacetime situation, where they had time to listen to me, then I probably wasn't going to be able to minister to them in war. I was very aware of the importance of that. I kept it very short and pithy.

Each regiment has its own prayer, a Regimental Collect, and the CO decided it would be good for the men to learn the Collect. I suppose partly for the collective act of saying it together, which is quite binding. But also just to give them a prayer that they knew. We made sure they knew the Lord's Prayer and we taught the Collect, and getting some 800 men to learn a prayer is obviously something that we don't normally do. The RSM took it on. It was quite wonderful; he said, "Aye, nae problem, Sir." Basically people were given two days to learn it, and if in two days' time they didn't know it, they couldn't sign out of barracks. They [used to] go through the Guardroom in Germany and book out, and you couldn't book out unless you could say the prayer,

1. Private Vincent Stott of A Company, the youngest British soldier in the Gulf. (*Mike Moore*)

2. Off to war, Lieutenant 'Dicky' Donovan, and Captains Steve Telfer and Angus McLeod depart from Werl for their flight to the Gulf, December, 1990. (*G Richardson*)

3. A parcel from home. Every Royal Scot received a parcel from the *Sunday Post* on arrival at Blackadder Camp in Al Jubayl (see page 40). *(G Richardson)*

4. One of B Company's Warriors undergoes a 'pack change' (a change of engine) with the aid of a Samson recovery vehicle operated by the REME Light Aid Detachment. *(R Walker)*

5. Captain Tony Restall of the Royal Army Pay Corps (top left), Paymaster for the Royal Scots Battle Group, holds a pay parade in a sand storm for Queen's Company, The Grenadier Guards. A vital receipt was swept away by the high wind, and was never seen again. (*G Richardson*)

6. 'Desert Thunder', an improvised lavatory at Battle Group Main HQ, one of the many that were constructed while the Royals were waiting to go into action. (*G Richardson*)

O - 1176 ↑
OMD 80
TS 10033 E /106
SL 12A / 741
25 LITRES
FOR EXPORT

7. A Queen's Own Highlander, on attachment to the Royals, opens a parcel from home. Lavatory paper was always welcome. (*The Royal Scots*)

and you had this amazing scene of people saying the Regimental Prayer in the Guardroom before going out. People would go off on runs and you'd hear sections or platoons off running and saying the Prayer while running. It was quite amazing.

Major Stephen Blakey, Padre

Regimental Collect of the Royal Scots (The Royal Regiment)

O Lord Jesus Christ, Who are the first and the last, grant, we pray Thee, that, as Thou hast promised to be with us even unto the end of the world, so may the Royal Scots be the first to follow Thee and the last to forsake Thee, Who art with the Father and the Holy Ghost, one God, world without end. Amen.

It was essential that the men acclimatize quickly on their arrival in the Gulf, and the fitter the men became the quicker this would happen. During the fitness training a careful watch was kept by the Battalion Medical Officer who ensured that every man knew the telltale signs of dehydration, which would become especially important when they went out to the desert.

The morning fitness training was followed by a personal briefing from the Commanding Officer. By-passing the usual chain of command, Colonel Johnstone saw this as a way of controlling the spread of rumours and ensuring that everyone was kept fully informed of what was happening, but inevitably the initial announcement that the Battalion was to go to Saudi Arabia, when relayed to at least one soldier's family, became garbled.

I had a mother arrive on my doorstep, literally within hours of us knowing about it, because [her son] had been on the phone to her saying we're going, and she decided to come with her children to see him. I think certain messages get lost in the transmission, and she obviously thought that's it, he was on his way. So she arrived and we then had this open day for her. [We] showed her all the vehicles; took the kids, and actually it was quite a nice relief for us. I think she left feeling that he couldn't be in better hands. Having arrived slightly hostile to us – "What are you doing to my seventeen-year-old son?" – she left feeling genuinely that we were well-prepared, and it served to remind us all that we were actually in a position to go to war.

Major Bryan Johnston

Oddly enough, although current regulations prevented soldiers under eighteen from serving in Northern Ireland,[3] there was nothing to stop them going to the Gulf. Among the seventeen-year-olds who were to go with the Battalion to Saudi Arabia was Private Vincent Stott of A Company, who was to be the youngest soldier serving in the Gulf.

Although the Battalion was at a high level of manning, it was not up to full strength for war and in particular for the Establishment and Order of Battle required for Operation GRANBY. A major change in the Battalion's structure was the temporary disbandment of C Company, whose officers and men were redeployed to A, B and Fire Support Companies.

The training became far more intense. For a start you had a full platoon and that made quite a change. Because you've got folk gone doing this, someone sent away to do that, you never [usually] have your full platoon. There you did. You had a full ORBAT; every single slot filled.

Lieutenant Colin Dougan, Commander, 3 Platoon, A Company

Additionally, some shuffling was necessary to ensure that the right people were in the right jobs. It was, as Iain Johnstone put it, "An opportunity to put your career on a back burner and get on with the task in hand".

Once we knew we were going to war, you could get rid of the dead wood, you could bring in these bright young things that were desperately keen to take on a corporal's job. You knew that he was capable, but the number of courses he'd done, the time [he'd] spent, wasn't quite right. That meant that the right people were moving to the right jobs. Not just at soldier level; the Colonel was doing exactly the same; he'd come and say to you regularly, "If you don't perform, you are on the bus," because there were people ringing him up saying, "I'll do the job!" The other thing was discipline. No Jock was going to be caught malingering or having had a few beers too many, because he would immediately have been castigated by his peer group. The Sergeant Major didn't need to say, "Sort yourself out".

Major Bryan Johnston

I found that I had very minimal discipline problems. I found a section talking once and they were getting on to a Jock for not doing his job. They were saying, "You're fucking up here; you're letting us down!" We were sitting back with the OC and I said, "There you go; there's Jocks telling Jocks what to do, that's what it's all about."

WO2 Dave Dickson, Company Sergeant Major,
Fire Support Company

On hearing that the Battalion was moving to the Gulf, some of the Royal Scots' officers who were away on courses, or on attachment to other units, immediately made plans to return to the fold only to be told to wait. It would be pointless for any one of them to abandon a posting or training course and then to find that they were not required and that a valuable career opportunity had been sacrificed needlessly.

One officer who was recalled, by the Commanding Officer himself, was Captain Dermot Fulton who, following in Iain Johnstone's footsteps, was on attachment to the Omani Armed Forces. A fluent Arabic speaker, he was to return as Battalion Intelligence Officer.

Lieutenant Wendy Smart, on attachment from the Women's Royal Army Corps, and the only female officer in the Battalion, was second-in-command of Fire Support

Company when the warning order was received, a job she would not be allowed to do in the Gulf. Because she was awaiting news of her next posting, Lieutenant Smart was told by the Commanding Officer that she would not be going to the Gulf. Within days, however, Colonel Johnstone changed his mind and she was offered the job of second-in-command of Headquarters Company prior to departure for Saudi Arabia.

I was due to be posted in March, and the Colonel had already said to me that if I got the posting I wanted, then I would go to my posting, if not then I would go with them to the Gulf. At the time I had been given the posting I wanted and so he said, "Fine, you'll go to that." So it didn't affect me, I was not going with them. The Colonel suddenly decided that he wished me to go. He just suddenly said one day, "I've decided that you're coming with us, do you mind?" To which I thought, "Well I don't think I've got a lot of choice!"

Lieutenant Wendy Smart

While the Order of Battle was being sorted out, a high priority was being given to the Battalion's fleet of vehicles so that they would be clean, serviced and repainted in desert camouflage in time for their imminent sea journey. This task was the responsibility of the Quartermaster (Technical), Major Waugh, who re-allocated some of them to suit the new Order of Battle, and to ensure that the Rifle Companies and Fire Support Platoons had the mobility they would need.

We actually went [to the Gulf] with what was known as the GRANBY establishment, which was in excess of the normal wartime establishment, which consequently gave us a lot more vehicles. For example, we finished up with seventeen additional Warriors and fourteen 432s, which belonged to the battalion but were given to other people within the battalion. Instead of having the normal three ambulances we finished up with ten. Each company had two ambulances, plus a donkey [M548], so they actually had four 432s in each company, whereas normally it's two.

There were two things we had to look at before we left. Going on feedback we were getting from the Staffords, the two problems that they'd come up against were: one, they thought that the established ambulances were insufficient for the expected casualties, so we increased each company's ambulance by another one, so that gave each company two ambulances.

The other problem they envisaged was the wheeled vehicle problem of re-supply. Because of the sand etc they were getting a lot of bogged-down vehicles, and the vehicles just could not get forward to resupply the Warrior companies, so we looked at that. We said, OK fine, we've got these spare 432s. Milan [Anti-Tank] Platoon in its entirety was going to be mounted in Warrior, the four MFCs [Mortar Fire Controllers] were going to be mounted in Warrior. So consequently it threw up four Sultans and four 432s as spare vehicles. So we decided that, to alleviate the resupply problem, we would give them a 432, which we stripped out completely. We then welded on to the top of it some water bowsers as well, so the interior could be used for ammunition and ration resupply and the exterior could be used for water resupply, and that was the only three things we were looking at.

The priority as far as we were concerned was ammunition, water, food, in that order. Consequently each [rifle] company finished up with that configuration of 432s. Because of [Fire Support Company's] resupply problem, we left the Mortar [Platoon] with an additional 432. We also gave Milan [Platoon] an additional 432, again to be used purely for ammunition and resupply.

When we got out there they then gave us some of these M548s, purely a load-carrying vehicle. It's a tracked steering unit and the rest of it is purely a load-carrying base. They were a one-off issue, to be used until they fell into the ground. There were no spares. We got four of those, so we dished those out to the companies purely as a resupply vehicle.

We were actually one hundred percent on the road, whereas the Staffords [when GRANBY I was announced] were nowhere near that, nor was anybody else. We remained in that very good position right through the lead-up to GRANBY and indeed right through GRANBY; we always had one hundred percent on the road.

In Germany it was different. We were very, very fortunate; we had a very good working relationship not just with the military aspect of Warrior, but with the civilian aspect of Warrior. I used to speak directly to London and get my spares and they'd take them off the supply line for me and stick them in the post, simple as that. So consequently from the point of view of having our equipment on the road ready to move, we were ready to sprint, and it wasn't just the Warrior aspect, the whole fleet was in good order. In fact we left one 432 in Werl and the reason for that was it had crashed that morning. As we were going down the road from the camp to put them on the train, it went off the road. Consequently we had to leave that one behind but [in] everything else we were ninety-nine point nine percent complete. In all respects, radio equipment, the lot, and remained so throughout.

The only thing which gave us any great problems whilst we were on GRANBY was the old Ferret. We started with five, and brought one back. I think everybody has a problem with Ferrets. It's one of those things that the infantry just doesn't seem to be able to maintain, try as we may. It's a liaison-type vehicle, it's not a fighting vehicle. Two I/C Headquarters Company had one. If you haven't got it, it puts a strain on something else. We eventually took the Ferrets off the Liaison people and gave them CVRTs which we had given to the Milan Platoon, which they weren't using really. So they finished up with those.

Major G. C. H. "Paddy" Waugh, Quartermaster, (Technical)

Work on the vehicles was largely carried out by the men who were to crew them, particularly the drivers who would be responsible for making sure that the routine maintenance was carried out when the Battalion was out in Saudi Arabia. The more each officer and man knew about his vehicle, the more likely it was that the vehicle would remain roadworthy during the coming battles.

There was a hell of a lot of work to be done. Because you were going, everyone started to take more interest I think. If you had a stoppage in your chain gun, your turret chain or whatever, that became rather important. If you had a bit missing from an engine, then that became extremely important. Then we had the gunnery Captains who were trained through Hohne. Oddly, all of us could fire, but the range staff were taken from another unit, and they must have felt as bad as we felt when we were in Bremerhaven. And the same thing for the soldiers at Sennelager. So we had the best training, because things were starting to become more for war as opposed to for safety. Although, don't get me wrong, the safety was still there, but people had to begin to realize that the drills they were learning now were drills that we would have to carry out for real. All the vehicle crews were up in Hohne; we [the platoon commanders] came back down and got the last half, I think, of the package at Sennelager, and then we were into getting the vehicles off. That was the big rush.

Lieutenant Colin Dougan

It was ironic that the vehicles were to receive their coating of desert-sand-coloured paint in the snow, and even that task had problems to be overcome.

We did it in two stages actually. Because we had to proof fire [the] 30mm [guns], all the Warriors had to go up to Hohne, so we set up two painting points. We had a painting point up at Hohne itself, where the Warriors and the CVRTs were put through, and then we had a painting session back down in Werl where we did the remainder, the 432s plus the B vehicle fleet. We achieved all our painting with the exception of two vehicles, two four-ton vehicles which we picked up when we were out there. We had to hand-paint those. Everything else was painted prior to departure. Again, because of the volume of paint which was demanded from the system, the system couldn't cope and consequently a lot of the paint was produced locally in Munster. With the volume of painting that was going on, the amount of spraying machines that we had, as a battalion, was insufficient, so again we had to do a trawl of other units to get sufficient paint-spraying machines, as we did with a lot of equipment.

Major Paddy Waugh

We went to Hohne, done a lot of field-firing and different shoots and taking out two different targets. One vehicle takes out the left one and the other takes out the right one and you've got to pump the three shots into them straight away and there's no mistaking, you've just got to do it. Straight after that the vehicles went into the sheds and we stayed up all night painting these vehicles with spray paint and all of our uniforms got all desert-paint-coloured. It was snowing; it was very very unrealistic circumstances. We just couldn't imagine a desert at that time. It was the strangest sight, after the vehicles had been painted, seeing them all rolling onto the range in a snowy background, and you had to imagine that you'd be in desert kit in a warm environment, and we were training for it in the snow!

Private Nick Williams, Reconnaissance Platoon

An unexpected bonus of the reunification of Germany was the opportunity for some of the vehicle crews at Hohne to inspect the Soviet-made equipment in use with the former East German Army, now called *Bundeswehr Ost*. Having spent many years training to fight the armed forces of the Warsaw Pact, it was with great interest that the Royals were allowed access to the sort of armoured vehicles they were likely to encounter in the Gulf – to climb inside them, to see them on the move, and even to see them through their own weapons sights. The vehicles were somewhat smaller and faster than expected and consequently would be difficult to pick up as targets, but one reassuring point was the comparative thinness of the armour, variously described as being like a "baked bean tin" or a "Kit-Kat wrapper". Certainly if they could hit the Iraqis' vehicles they could destroy them.

That came at a very good time actually, we were limited to what we saw. We saw a few tanks, a few armoured personnel carriers, particularly the MTLB and the T55 tank. Those were the two main ones we looked at. You could spend ages and ages looking at videos of the parades in Red Square in Moscow and so on, of all these vehicles, but until you actually stand next to them you don't appreciate their size. In particular the MTLB, which is the personnel carrier, was so small, and the BMP which is another personnel carrier, so small, the silhouette is tiny, tiny. I'm six [feet] two, and I was standing next to this MTLB and my head is parallel with the roof and that's a small vehicle! Difficult to acquire [as a target] when it's moving fast, and it moves fast, especially the BMP.

Lieutenant Guy Richardson

While the Coalition forces were assembling in Saudi Arabia world Press watched and anticipated. Was this to be the beginning of World War Three? In the absence of any information from more reliable sources, the outpourings of Saddam Hussein were mulled over, and added fuel to the wild speculation. His predictions of massive numbers of casualties led the Press to draw parallels with the great battles of the First World War, ignoring the fact that, at least as far as the Coalition ground forces were concerned, it would be armoured warfare on a massive scale in ideal terrain against Soviet weapons systems. In short it was what the British Army on the Rhine had been training for since the end of the Second World War. However, the fact remains that because the infantrymen were to be deployed in vehicles, mostly with a full complement of ten, there was a distinct possibility of higher casualties than normally occur amongst infantry. It is not difficult to calculate that a missile hitting a Warrior would, in all probability, result in the death of all ten occupants, whereas it would almost certainly take more than ten, even well-aimed, shots to kill the same number of men deployed on the ground.

In addition, there was the unknown element of the Iraqis' stock of what have come to be known as "weapons of mass destruction". Certainly, it was very likely that chemical and nerve agents would be used, and the possibility of a nuclear strike, however unwise, could not at this stage be ruled out.

During November Brigadier Patrick Cordingley, Commander of 7 Brigade, entertained some journalists at his camp in Saudi Arabia and, speaking candidly in response to a question, he remarked that what was abundantly clear was that, if two armies of that size met, there must inevitably be a large number of casualties. Although he was speaking off the record, the ever-watchful Press eagerly seized upon this unguarded remark, misinterpreted it and exaggerated it out of all proportion.

While the Royals continued their training, paying extra attention to First Aid, so that any man in the Battalion could save a comrade's life, the ill-informed debate in the media about the prospect of high casualties continued. It was dealt with in various ways by the Royal Scots, and even regarded with some grim humour within the Battalion.

On one occasion we were listening to a BBC radio programme on the Services' station in Germany, and they had a talk-in, and the question was about casualty figures. What was the acceptable figure for casualties in the Gulf? This chap came on and he didn't see any problem with forty per cent. Forty per cent would have been justifiable, no problem at all. The interviewer said, "You obviously know quite a great deal about this. Are you a military man yourself?" He said, "No, I'm a plumber," and we could just imagine this chap turning away at the S-bend there with his torque wrench, saying, "Forty per cent, fifty per cent if necessary!"
Captain Robert Bruce, Second-in-Command, A Company

Things like NBC training, medical training, and all the rest of it became fairly high on the priority list. If you didn't do your NBC properly you would die, and if you didn't get your medical training someone else would die.

My mind didn't dwell on the thought of taking casualties, the thought of one of the vehicles being hit was always [there]. You didn't think of losing a limb, living with excruciating pain, crutches for the rest of your life. You think of either coming out for "tea and medals" which was one of the big expressions at the time, or dead, and as long as I was going to have one or the other, I really didn't mind, but I didn't want to come out either a vegetable or an invalid.

What's the point thinking about death? You've got to think more positively.

Lieutenant Colin Dougan

One of my major fears was how I would react. If we lost ten vehicles, a hundred men, and we withdrew to the next position there would then be a time of reorganization. Colonel Iain would be looking to me as one of the prime movers in that reorganization, having time to get people jollied up and to deal with people's concerns and focus in on what's to be done and deal with grief issues and the pain issues.

One of my major fears was how was I going to do that? Why should I not be cracked up if other people are cracked up? That worried me quite a lot. Fortunately it never happened.

Major Stephen Blakey

The Battalion's Regimental Aid Post grew from its peace-time establishment of one Doctor and seven Regimental Medical Assistants (RMAs), to two Doctors, one Ambulance Controller, five RMAs, four Combat Medical Technicians from the RAMC, two Radio Operators, sixteen Bandsmen (as stretcher-bearers) and some additional drivers. Although, in theory, all the medical personnel were highly trained, the bandsmen were not, and everyone was put through additional training, paying particular attention to NBC medicine. The medical supplies were also reassessed. Now that there were two Doctors, the North-west Europe scale on issue was doubled and, because they were going to the Gulf, fluid supplies were further increased. Eventually the medical centre was stripped of everything that might come in useful.

Although the threat of NBC weapons had been on the agenda for a war in Europe, somehow the threat from the Iraqis was more real. The Royals only had to look at the newspapers for graphic evidence of the Iraqis' use of poison gas against the Kurds.

One thing I had at the back of my mind was that if you are going to die in war, [if] you are going to die for your country, then you may as well do it being brave and leading men in battle. That's what I joined the Army and the Infantry for, to lead men on operations. Although I certainly had no intention nor desire to be suicidal about it, what wouldn't be at all acceptable and what was in us all at the back of our minds was the NBC, the chemical threat, whereby we could be miles out of contact, across the other side of the border, never having been committed to any assault and end up dying in a pretty painful way, in an undistinguished sort of way, as a result of a chemical strike.

Captain Robert Bruce

A lot of time was therefore devoted to NBC training. Each day for a set amount of time everyone had to wear NBC kit to become accustomed to working in the hot and bulky outfit with its clumsy boots and gloves. The only difference was that this was winter in Germany and the temperature was nowhere near the heat that the Royals would have to deal with in the Gulf.

Inevitably, trying to keep on top of the massive workload while observing the NBC training routine produced its lighter moments.

I was talking to people in London [on the telephone] with my respirator on, "You sound a bit funny". "Aye I am a bit fucking funny, I've got my respirator on!"

Major Paddy Waugh

NBC is a very difficult thing in the Army because we try to do it for real, we try to take it seriously, and these guys go off for NBC Instructors and they come back and they're full of enthusiasm, but it's such an unpleasant thing to do that no one can get excited about it. When the Gulf thing began we did take it seriously and we had these sections during the day [when respirators had to be worn] I used to try and be out of the barracks at the time, to go and visit a family! But we had to do it because obviously it was one of the biggest worries we had.

Major Stephen Blakey

Two formalities had to be attended to before the soldiers went to the Gulf. Each man had to have a valid ten-year passport, and everyone had to sign a mobilization declaration under the Army Acts before going to war.

I think when it finally sunk in with my soldiers was when they were signing the declaration. In as much as they were under orders to go to war. I explained exactly what the declaration was and that if they did go absent or anything like that they'd be done for desertion, and the consequences of that because they were going to war, and the Company went strangely quiet. You could see it in the lads' faces when they were signing it, it was sinking in, "My God, this is it, I'm signing something here that I'm going to war!"

Warrant Officer 2 Dave Dickson

So that the soldiers could spend more time saying farewell to their families, the whole Battalion was given a long weekend leave before the departure for the Gulf began. As luck would have it, the weather closed in and some of the Royals had a nightmare journey home, in the snow, and some found it difficult to say farewell to their families and friends.

Friday 7 December, 1990: Finally our pre-Gulf leave has arrived. Leave is not really the word for it as we are just having a long weekend but it is well-deserved as we have all been working long hours over the past month since we have been warned off for a definite tour of the Gulf. In fact we had last Sunday off work on returning from Sennelager and this has been the only day off in the last three weeks. The vehicle crews who were at Hohne did not even get last Sunday off! The morning was spent entirely on admin and the Coy was fallen out at 1330 hrs. The married soldiers had local leave and the single Jocks had coaches laid on back to Edinburgh.

Saturday 8 December, 1990: After getting the ferry from Zeebrugge, we arrived in Dover at 2300. I had an hour and a half sleep on the ferry before setting off for Northumberland. We made very good time before the weather closed in. Snow worsened by strong wind made driving impossible (20mph on A2). We stopped at a service station at 0300 as the weather was so bad. Will weather improve or worsen? We decided to carry on at 0430. The weather cleared just N of M62 Jn. Arrived Ponteland at 0700.

2nd Lieutenant Roger M. Walker, Commander, 6 Platoon, B Company

I'd heard lots of things, like when the war starts we're only going to have half an hour to live, so I thought I'd better spend as much cash as I can now, have a good time while I can. It was a very bad feeling. We had a short two-day leave before we went to the Gulf and it was really bad, having to leave your family behind, and you didn't know whether or not you were going to see them [again] and everyone was in tears. It just wasn't my scene at all. All my friends were shaking my hand and stuff like that, which had never happened before, it was just a really bad time.

Private Williams

At least one soldier found the return journey complicated also.

Major Soutar actually said before we left, "It looks like you will be going to war." He was telling us, "Bring knives with you." On the leave we got prior to going to the Gulf, due to no fault of my own, I missed my connection to get back on to the bus, so phoned up, made my way down to London. In London, the Military Police came and collected me and I was taken – I forget the name of the building, dealing with the travel arrangements for the whole of the British Army. They put me on a flight because I told them I was off to the Gulf. I got stopped by the Transport Police with this knife at the bottom of my bag. I had to explain to them why. He says, "Just stick it at the bottom, but if you get to the other side [and] you get caught, say we don't know anything about it!"

Private Mark Morrice, Quartermaster's Platoon

At last the departure for the Gulf was imminent and the Battalion bade its farewell to its BAOR Commanders, some of whom themselves were off to Saudi Arabia.

We had Brigadier Bob McAfee as the Brigade Commander at that stage and he came on his farewell and I'll never forget we all crowded into the gymnasium and he gave us a remarkably short succinct, punchy, pre-departure from Germany, speech. He was going out to join General de la Billière. He finished his speech saying, "And we'll send them homewards tae think again!", and the Jocks just roared. It almost brought the roof down, and he sort of turned and went off. If we could have fixed bayonets then, we could have marched all the way to Kuwait City.

Major Bryan Johnston

The Battalion's journey to Saudi Arabia was effectively in two parts. First the vehicles and stores were sent off on their long sea voyage, then the officers and men followed by air. The Advance Party, led by Major Johnston, who was at that time acting Second-in-Command of the Battalion as well as Commander of Fire Support Company, flew out on 10 December. The day the Advance Party left for the Gulf, Major Kirk Gillies arrived at Albuhera Barracks to take over as Second-in-Command.

I was between postings. I was short-toured in Cyprus; dragged back, and I arrived in Germany on 10 December. I underwent all forms of agony to get myself sorted out and fit. I had never seen a Warrior in my life.

I flew [my wife] back to the UK, and almost said "Cheerio", to her at the airport, "See you next year with any luck!" and that was it.

Major Kirk Gillies, Second-in-Command

On 21 December the Commanding Officer, Second-in-Command and the Company Commanders flew out and, over a period of about three weeks, the main body of the Jocks, with their respective Platoon Commanders.

We flew out on Caledonian Airways, Tristar from Hanover, and we were looked after tremendously. It was nice to go out to war with Scottish stewardesses saying goodbye to you. Lots of tartan. They looked after us well, I'll say no more than that. We actually went out over a period of about three to four weeks. What you do is you send out your logistics side to set things up, then your command structure and then, because the vehicles had gone by ship, we needed to have drivers and commanders to take the vehicles off the ships, and to work on them. Then, once they'd got to the desert, the soldiers in the back of the vehicles would marry up with them there. I personally spent a lot of time hanging around Al Jubayl sorting a lot of stuff out.

Captain Neil Brownlie, Operations Officer

Those fortunate enough to fly with a civilian airline enjoyed the benefit of the in-flight entertainment and attractive stewardesses, and for a lucky few there was even a chance to drink a last beer in the transit lounge during the stop to refuel in Cyprus.

Sunday, December 30, 1990: Up at 7.30. Kit on. Phoned Dad for last time. Paraded 0900. Left for Hanover airport. Flight on Tristar – B.Cal! – via Akrotiri in Cyprus to Dharan. Left Germany at 1400 on the start of our Great Adventure to Arabia. B.Cal. service was very good – the usual airline meals etc. & in-flight films, finishing with *The Jungle Book* just as we touched down. What a way to arrive – one of my favourite films of all. Wonderful!

2nd Lieutenant Roger Walker

Some of the men, however, went over on the more spartan RAF flights which flew non-stop and landed at the military airfield. Even if they hadn't felt that they were on their way to war during the flight, as they landed and the scale of the operation unfolded before them they certainly did.

The thing that really hit home was the Huey, the American Huey helicopters hovering roughly about twenty feet from the ground actually giving us close protection, and that's when it really hit home. We werenae' expecting to see that, we thought we were just going to get off at an airport, through the hanger, on the big trucks and away we go.

Private John Drain, 1 Platoon, A Company

Chapter 2

A SINGLENESS OF PURPOSE

We had four weeks to get operationally ready as a Brigade, there was no time to fart about with floppy hats and desert boots and all that sort of stuff. We had to train with a singleness of purpose. Everything that we did, everything that we trained, for was geared towards one object and that was the eventual engagement and destruction of the Iraqi ground forces. To some people it came as a bit of a shock that we took things so very seriously. There was a [staff officer] who thought that we were taking it too seriously. He commented that I had too rigid, too spartan a régime for my men. I told him to fuck off!

Major John Potter

On its arrival in Saudi Arabia the Battalion had until the end of January to reach operational readiness. This included honing the soldiers' individual battle skills and building up the training from Section, through Platoon, to full-scale Company attacks using live ammunition, by day and by night, as well as vehicle movement at all levels from Platoon up to Division. An important point to consider was that resources used up in training would not be available for the ground war, so certain types of ammunition had to be conserved, and some exercises were combined with essential tactical moves to lessen wear and tear on the engines and reduce the likelihood of vehicles breaking down in action. Patrick Cordingley's 7 Brigade had been in theatre for nearly three months so there was a lot of catching up to be done. But the men of 4 Brigade would not have to break so much new ground and could learn valuable lessons from 7 Brigade's experience so far.

The Royal Scots' Advance Party had been given the task of establishing who was who and what was where, so that the Commanding Officer could be given a thorough update on the current situation and so that the arrival of the Battalion could be effected without any difficulty. But the initial contact was surprising.

One extraordinary incident was [when] I went for my intelligence briefing. I was wearing my Glengarry, as if to say the Jocks have arrived sort of thing. There was a great feeling amongst the ones that were there [that] now we could really get down to business. I went to see the chap in the Intelligence Briefing, and this chum that I knew wasn't there, but there was a Captain there, and he was briefing this civilian who had on a Free Kuwait T-shirt. They were chatting and pointing to the map etc. This young sergeant came up and said, "Yes, can I help you Sir?" I said, "Yea, I wonder if there's a chance of getting a quick briefing, I arrived at theatre yesterday and I just want a quick update." He said, "Well, the Captain's busy just now." This Captain cut away from his board and said to me, "I can't deal with you now. You'll have to wait until your Brigade arrives, and do it through the chain of command."

My Brigade wasn't due for about a month or so at that stage, and so I was slightly indignant. I then went and found my friend and said, "Who's the civvie he's briefing?" So this chum of mine, a fellow Major, went across there. It turned out to be some local expatriate who was working in the oil industry, who'd come in to see his chum and he was getting the whole brief, whilst there was I, a pukka, bona fide Advance Party, couldn't get [any information]. So immediately this guy was put in the picture and his civvie chum was thrown out of the Headquarters.

Major Bryan Johnston

No sooner had the transport aircraft touched down in Saudi Arabia than the Royals were given bottled water to drink.

Although there was little danger of anyone becoming dehydrated, for the weather was dull and windy, at every turn they were offered yet more water. They were taken by bus to Blackadder Camp[1] where they were given a meal, yet more bottled water to drink, and a parcel from the *Edinburgh Sunday Post*.

They also received their first set of desert camouflage "combats" complete with the black desert rat insignia of the 4th Armoured Brigade on the right sleeve and such essentials as sunburn cream, even though it was cold and overcast. The Jocks were somewhat confused by this, because it was winter in Saudi Arabia. But although the temperature at night plummeted, once they were out in the desert they would soon experience the fierce heat of the midday sun.

They were told to rest until transport came to take them out to their vehicles in the desert. The intention was to get the men out as soon as possible so that training could begin, and so that they could take part in any necessary defence of the region, for there still seemed a possibility that Saddam Hussein might send his forces into Saudi Arabia.

The Battalion's move to the Gulf took place over Christmas and the New Year so most of the men were still in Werl at Christmas, but by 31 December a good number had arrived in the Gulf. Hogmanay celebrations were, however, fairly low key, although there was a Piper and, it has been admitted, a toast for a lucky few with some unblessed Communion wine cajoled from the Padre. Most made do with alcohol-free beer, and many turned in before midnight, conscious that the next day was a working day and therefore an early start.

31 December, 1990: The Jocks in my tent bought some alcohol-free beer from NAAFI to celebrate New Year. There was not much festive feeling and we were all packed and asleep by 1000.

1 January, 1991: Happy New Year! Reveille at 0600 – without

a hangover. That time on 1 Jan I am normally going to bed not getting up.

2nd Lieutenant Roger Walker

The Padre arrived on 27 December, having made the decision to spend Christmas in Werl where most of the Jocks were. There had been some controversy about sending Chaplains out with the troops to Saudi Arabia, but, provided some discretion was exercised during the brief stay at Al Jubayl, there was no real problem.

We were told quite simply to be sensible. While you were in Al Jubayl it would have been quite easy to offend the locals, so we just didn't do things terribly in public. We didn't hide what we were doing, and there was one occasion where if people had wanted, if they'd had binoculars, they could have seen us holding a Christian Service. But there wasn't any overt pressure. I think there'd been a long wrangle between the Foreign and Commonwealth Office and the Ministry of Defence about it, because initially Chaplains weren't going. They'd said, "No Chaplains". They then said that Chaplains could go, but should be called Welfare Officers. Our Chaplain General, he's a very strong character, defended our cause all the way, and my position was defended by the Geneva Convention, that as a Chaplain I have special rights and access to prisoners and so on. If I don't identify myself as a Chaplain, I have no rights at all, I am just an unarmed person. So in order to maintain our position within the Geneva Convention we had to go as Chaplains wearing our crosses, [and] our rank. If I went into shops and so on, I'd turn my collar inside out so that people wouldn't see my crosses, because I didn't want to offend, but apart from that really I didn't do much else.

Major Stephen Blakey

As the New Year dawned, with it came the rain. The Jocks were to be taken out to the desert to rendezvous with their vehicles but, after all their hours of preparation in the garages at Werl and Hohne, there was a problem. Some of the vehicles had not yet arrived.

The problem we had, which was a bit frustrating from the lads' point of view and from my point of view, was [that] I had to reissue the whole of A Company's vehicles. Because of the time-lag with having left Germany, put them on the boats at Bremerhaven, and the time that they would have been expected to arrive in Riyadh, it just did not work in with the plot. So consequently we actually went into the War Reserve and drew up another seventeen or eighteen vehicles out of War Reserve to give A Company their complete fourteen, B Company I think were down two and Queen's Company were down one, something like that. These were still on the boats, still on the high seas. It made no difference, a vehicle is a vehicle, the only thing is it's never quite the same, it's not your vehicle and having spent all that time at Hohne zeroing and cracking on, we had to go through that process again with the A Company vehicles, that again was a bit of time misspent shall we say.

Major Paddy Waugh

From the outset, very strict discipline was imposed, and continuing the uncompromising attitude adopted during the preparations in Werl, the Battalion was very obviously preparing for war.

I think it's fair to say we took it as being for real from the time we actually set foot in Saudi. That didn't actually sink in, or didn't seem to sink in with other people. *Yes*, we were going to go.

A couple of occasions:

The Brigade Commander was giving an "O" Group in early February, and he said to the whole Brigade, "We are now doing Stand-To and wearing helmets in Brigade Headquarters." We'd been doing that in the Royal Scots from the time we landed! This was some big new event for Brigade Headquarters.

The other one: George Lowder [the Adjutant] and I were going to Brigade HQ, and we went in, as the Royal Scots did, our full webbing on, our helmets, our rifles, and all our kit with us for the day. And we were met with this classic remark, "Oh my God, not more Royal Scots carrying grenades around with them!" These people were wandering around Brigade carrying a pistol and not much else, and we were wearing NBC suit and full webbing. It was a completely different attitude. We were playing it for real from day one. They didn't seem to click into that until much closer than actual G-Day.

Captain Dermot Fulton, Intelligence Officer

We imposed very strict light discipline and very strict clothing discipline, in as much as everybody carried all their kit all the time and we didn't allow anybody to drive [looking] out of the turrets, they all had to be closed down. Those fundamental lessons we worked at very very hard. It made life very difficult, but by the time we were going to war it was just second nature. If I saw a vehicle in the desert; if it didn't have a windscreen, it was mine, and if it was driving closed down, it was mine, because I don't think anybody else really bothered too much.

We didn't allow any recreation within our area, so there were no volleyball pitches, there were no showers, no videos and no electricity. Our tactical area was just that, it was a tactical area. Other units did all sorts of things, that we refused to do, like having officers' guest nights and things like that.

Lt.Colonel Iain Johnstone

The full battle-load of a Warrior left no room for luxuries. Soon the priority would be to pack as much ammunition into the vehicles as possible, and consequently everyone's kit had to be reduced. Much of what was not needed was "backloaded" (sent back through the rear echelons) to be retrieved later, but some kit was even buried or burnt. Eventually each man, including the Commanding Officer, had pared his belongings down to the absolute minimum.

The officers lived in exactly the same way as all the men. We stripped the vehicles down very early on, so that even I was sharing a Bergen with two other people, and we threw away absolutely everything that was not instrumental in the destruction of Iraqis. The only things that we allowed people to keep were washing and shaving kit, a spare set of clothes, a short wave radio in the vehicle, somewhere, and perhaps a boogie box.[2] Everything else was shared.

Lt.Colonel Iain Johnstone

Space in the vehicles was very very limited indeed and the only things we had inside the vehicles were ammunition, water and rations, so we had to strap tins on to the outside of the waggon. Because space was limited, we only carried the minimum of dress that we could cope with.

Things like green combat jackets which we brought out got thrown away; roll mats which were insulating mats you sleep on, those all got burnt. We threw away the vehicle crew helmets and just kept our battle helmets. We trimmed out everything. I burned a number of T-shirts, half of my socks [and] half of my underpants. At that stage we'd been issued our second set of combats, after a month, and so we kept two sets of combats, three pairs of socks, three T-shirts, three pairs of underpants, washing and shaving kit, towel, sleeping bag and your stand-up fighting kit. And that was basically it, apart from perhaps a couple of books.

2nd Lieutenant Roger Walker

We then arrived at the vehicles. At the start it wasn't so bad because you [didn't get] "bombed up" straight away, and you could have a bit of room. But as soon as all the kit came into the waggon, that's when stuff started getting burned and thrown away. You lived on one article of cold weather [clothing], I had one sweat shirt, apart from my normal uniform, that would have been there for cold weather. So luckily it wasnae' that cold, except at night.

Private David Gibb, Signaller, 2 Platoon, A Company

When they were not actively training, the soldiers led a spartan existence, in and around their vehicles. Such luxuries as having a hot shower and using a proper lavatory would be rarely experienced, except when the men were lucky enough to spend a day at A2 Echelon on rest and recreation.

It was the same for every single day, the same routine. About five, six, you'd get half an hour Stand-To in your trenches, then you'd come out, a couple of people would get the breakfast ready, so that you'd clean your weapons right away. We always cleaned our weapons about twice a day, because of the sand getting in the mechanism. We lived right next to the vehicle, slept beside it under big Cam nets running off the vehicle, just like a tent. We slept under this, sometime we weren't allowed out of it. So you're always in there getting all your admin; checking out; always checking the webbing, make sure you've got everything; your ammunition, make sure it's working properly; weapons, making sure there's nothing wrong with them, and just doing vehicle maintenance as well.

All the time we had vehicle checks, it was the driver that organized it, rather than the commander, because he knew everything about Warrior. So he detailed people to do certain things. Food was quite tight. It was just ration packs we were getting. You get your ten-man ration packs. A ration pack would have burgers, curries, things like that, so it was all right, you got used to it. We all mucked in; we had a roster. Some guys would do the washing up; you had your few that couldn't cook at all, so people would do the dishes, people would clear the food, people would tidy up, so it was just mucking in.

Private Vincent Stott, 2 Platoon, A Company

The decision to feed the Battalion mainly on pre-packed rations was taken as a precautionary measure. The only sure way of avoiding outbreaks of illness, which could have seriously affected the Battalion's capacity to train and fight[3], would be to limit the men's intake of locally produced fresh rations. Every precaution was taken to prevent the possible spread of disease and to make everyone aware of the potential danger from insect bites or stings.

The desert itself is very clean, and by meticulous rubbish control and by burning out things, burning out the latrines every day, if not two times, three times a day, we kept down the problem of flies and so on. There was the odd scorpion I think. Once the chaps had tired of digging out scorpions to have contests to see who could get the biggest one, then we just ignored them. I don't think anyone got stung by one. People meticulously checked inside their sleeping bags before they got into them, shook their boots out and so on. Basically if you left them alone, they left you alone.

Major John Potter

A normal day would be, getting up, Stand-To, usually first light, start the morning routine, wash and shave, maybe do some training, check the traps. We used to put wee traps out for scorpions and things; we caught a couple of large dung beetles; we used to have beetle races. It all depended on the day; sometimes it was really bad weather, raining. I'd been in the desert three days and it rained!

Private Scott Gillies, Mortar Platoon, Fire Support Company

Once the Royal Scots Battle Group had assembled in the desert it was a completely self-contained fighting force, with a "tail", the A and B Echelons, which provided logistical support. The Warrior-borne Armoured Infantry initially consisted of A and B Companies of the Royal Scots, and Queen's Company of the Grenadier Guards, each of three platoons. However, during the large-scale exercises and for the actual ground war, the Grenadier Guards were sent off to the 14th/20th Hussars Battle Group, and the Royal Scots were joined by A Squadron, the Life Guards.

Commander of A Company, of the Royal Scots, was Major Norman Soutar. At 30, with a local promotion, he was the youngest Major, if not the youngest company commander, in the Gulf. Major Soutar led from the front and had a reputation for fitness which was echoed by his Company; unofficially known by the Jocks as "SAS Company". B Company was commanded by Major John Potter, on attachment from the Royal Highland Fusiliers. He had some of the toughest street-fighters in the Battalion under his command, but his skill in man-management enabled him to maintain loyalty and discipline without compromising their fighting spirit. Fire Support Company, commanded by Major Bryan Johnstone a King's Own Scottish Borderer, who took the Advance Party to the Gulf, consisted of the Reconnaissance, Anti-Tank and Mortar Platoons. Major Johnston was about to go to Staff College when the Battalion was notified that it was off to the Gulf. The only way he could stay with the Battalion and go to the Gulf was to offer his resignation, effective from their return, and this he did. Fire Support Company was effectively dispersed throughout the Battle Group. The Reconnaissance Platoon, as its name implies, normally worked forward of the Battle Group, reconnoitring the terrain, locating routes and enemy formations. The Anti-tank Platoon provided a section for each Company, and included a mobile section which could be used wherever necessary. To bring it up to its full GRANBY Order of Battle, it was joined by a Milan section from the Queen's Own Highlanders, which was attached to Queen's Company, the Grenadier Guards. The Mortar Platoon's job was to provide covering fire for the whole Battle Group, and Mortar Fire Controllers (MFCs) travelled with the Rifle Companies to direct mortar fire as it was needed.

The Mortar Platoon is an entity unto itself. It travels in two halves, so you've got covering fire. We worked with two MFCs so one section can go firm and cover one company, the other section can go firm and cover the other company. But we work by ourselves. We can be four and a half Ks away from the company to give them covering fire.

Private Scott Gillies

Each key position within the Battalion was covered by a "step-up" – a person who could take over the job if the incumbent was killed or wounded. Colonel Johnstone's place, for instance, would be taken by his Second-in-Command, Major Kirk Gillies, and within each company, platoon and section every weapon and every piece of equipment could be operated by almost any member.

You've got Main Headquarters; the majority of your communications assets are there, and they rumble along behind, and then you've got Tac [Tactical] Headquarters, which is where the Commanding Officer positions himself, between the two forward companies and the Alternative or step-up Headquarters, which leap-frogs if necessary and is ready to take over. If we were giving orders formally we would all join together. The Main Headquarters would catch up with us, or we would stop and let them catch up with us and we would then give orders in the Main Headquarters complex.

I commanded the Alternative Headquarters. My job, in war, was to be prepared to stand in for the CO at any time. Now there are various ways you can play that. You can either go back to the Main Headquarters and sit in that. Main Headquarters sort of rumbles along about five kilometres behind the battle. But George Lowder, the Adjutant [who ran Main HQ] was a very competent chap so there was absolutely no point in me interfering there. So I rumbled along no more than about three hundred metres behind Colonel Iain, keeping his pennant in sight, so I was current with the battle at all times. I had exactly the same radio net, so I could listen to the Brigade and the Battalion net, and I could hear exactly what he was saying. By doing that, by being up with the CO, if he'd been hit, I'd have seen it straight away. I could have taken over, and I was able to read the battle and perhaps assist. The danger was that I was perhaps too close and therefore in danger of being taken out as well, but that was the risk you took.

Major Kirk Gillies

Keeping the Battle Group mobile and completely supplied with everything from men, ammunition, fuel, food and water, to mail and parcels from home was the responsibility of the Echelons. A1 Echelon was solely concerned with fuel supply. A2 Echelon had a wider remit, it provided virtually everything else in the military sense, with particular emphasis on maintaining the Battle Group's ability to fight.

Keeping the vehicles mobile, as we have already seen, was the responsibility of the Quartermaster (Technical), who was assisted by a Light Aid Detachment (LAD) from the Royal Electrical and Mechanical Engineers (REME).

Obtaining spares, however, was difficult initially because everything had to be accounted for properly before it could be issued, and the units responsible for doing this did not have sufficient manpower for this massive task. The phrase "In theatre but not yet visible" was coined to describe material that was in store but had not yet been entered on the computer, so could not be issued.

My main concern from the QM Tech's point of view on leaving Germany was the lack of spares. Which was more frustrating by knowing that the spares and all the equipment was there, but you couldn't get your bloody hands on it. Op GRANBY took precedence over everything at that stage. The problem was that the RAOC [Royal Army Ordnance Corps], God bless their cotton socks, had not envisaged the demand and supply problem they were going to get. So consequently when the supplies started to come in, they just couldn't control it. They were desperately undermanned; they finished up with good old Royal Pioneer Corps guys. I finished up giving them guys to help them out. I used to go round and you could see the kit, but you couldn't get it.

Major Paddy Waugh

It was quite likely that the Battle Group would be unable to stop frequently for replenishment when and if a ground war started, so each vehicle had to carry the maximum load, also the differences in performance and range of the three main tracked vehicles on issue had to be taken into account.

We worked out, with the terrain etc, the amount of fuel that A1 Echelon could carry, what the Warrior, CVRT and 432 could carry itself in its tanks and in its jerry cans. We then worked out, as a first line reserve, the amount of fuel which one of the 548s could carry which gave an additional number of miles and from that we ascertained that, from go to *stop*, the Battle Group could go for seventy-two hours, completely self-contained, with ammunition, water, rations and fuel without the need for A1 or A2 Echelon. That was the plan that we went for.

It got slightly fucked up, and I will use that word, by 4 Brigade itself, who insisted, and it was insist, that they would take half our jerry cans off us. Which they did. We had taken every jerry can that we could with us from Germany as we were instructed to do so, and at the same time, as soon as we got there we started building up a stock, whereas other battalions and other regiments hadn't bothered taking what they should have done in the first instance and thought, "Who wants jerry cans anyway?" We were a little bit miffed. Fortunately it didn't affect us, because of the distances travelled and for the time that we were travelling anyway. It didn't affect us, but it could have done.

Major Paddy Waugh

The essential lifeline between the Battalion in the desert and the families in Werl, and indeed those in Scotland, was maintained by the Assistant Adjutant, Lieutenant Bill Sutherland. With twenty years' experience in the Battalion's administrative office, he was ideally suited to running B2 Echelon in Al Jubayl, but during the weeks prior to the advance into Iraq he made the long drive north to visit the Battle Group as frequently as he could.

When the fighting started, Bill Sutherland would have the unenviable task of keeping track of the expected casualties through the Field Record Office, and ensuring that the official message of condolence from the Ministry of Defence was followed up by a telephone call from Saudi Arabia, and visits by Captain Mike Low, the Battalion Families Officer[4].

Fortunately the majority of the traffic flowing through Bill Sutherland's well-oiled clerical machine was the massive amount of "bluies" – soldiers' letters, and parcels, sent by the soldiers to and from their families. Another of Bill Sutherland's tasks was Press and PR Officer, and as a result he once received a complaint from a soldier's wife, who suggested that her husband, who had been interviewed by the media, could have been better employed writing a letter home! However, the tremendous support received by the soldiers from their families and from well-wishers all over Britain contributed greatly to the Battalion's morale.

We had tons of parcels and letters. I think it was just fantastic. I've never seen support like that, and it was very humbling in many ways. I think it's incredibly important if you feel that everybody back at home is on your side and thinks you are doing a wonderful job. It makes your life very much easier. I would have hated to have done that in the atmosphere of the Americans in Vietnam for instance, where they were getting hate letters. It made my life very much easier.

Lt.Colonel Iain Johnstone

Many letters came through the BFPO 3000 scheme whereby mail could be addressed to "A Soldier (many were addressed to 'A Scottish Soldier') in the Gulf". Their distribution was assisted by the Padre, who ensured that every man had regular mail, even if he was not receiving letters from his family. Eventually the Padre and his driver, Private Butcher, even ran a small shop from their Landrover.

We ran a little shop. I would set the shop up, and people would come to buy cards, chocolate bars, cigarettes or lighters. We had battery shavers which were quite popular, all sorts of things, and if people wanted to talk to me they could come without anybody wondering what they were doing, and we'd have a chat. [Private] Butcher would take over the shop and I would go behind the vehicle and chat to people.

We started off, just with little odds and ends. The men spent a little time in Al Jubayl, then went straight out into the desert and were there for three months. They would see me go backwards and forwards and would ask, "Any chance of getting some cans of coke or a couple of Mars bars. Can you do this for me?", and that grew to a level where we would actually stock up on all sorts of things and try to respond to people's needs.

The NAAFI produced brochures for various things that you could do and one was Interflora. But really it was all arranged in such a way for the individual to go over to the NAAFI themselves and order the flowers. All of our lads were out in the desert, so we spoke to NAAFI [and] I became an Interflora agent. We drew our own forms up; soldier-proof forms. We rounded the money to reasonable amounts and we sent – I can't remember the numbers, but it was five [or] six hundred flower-orders home during the time and for St Valentine's Day.

We did things like organizing the desert bear – some organization that produces various cuddly toys in Army uniform, produced a bear in desert combats and you could get him in different headgear – you could get it with the TOS [Tam O'Shanter] with the Royal Scot patch and these became big favourites, and again on that we just photocopied the form. We converted the UK rate into Ryals [and] took all these orders. At one stage we had two thousand pounds worth of orders, and went to the field post office and said, "I need two thousand pounds worth of postal orders", not realizing that the biggest they had was twenty pounds, so I needed a hundred twenty-pound postal orders and of course there was the commission!

We lost a lot of money there, but we got a discount on all our NAAFI stock and made a little bit of money on that so it all balanced out.

Major Stephen Blakey

On 5 January the Platoon Commanders received their first tactical briefing. The next day they talked their Section Commanders through the tactics, which had been devised by the senior Battle Group commanders.

The tactics used by the sections of Jocks in the vehicles were well-practised. Each man knew precisely where he was to go as he jumped out of the back of the vehicle, and the two half sections supported each other as they moved forward with further fire support from the vehicle.

8. Corporal Derek Notman displays some of the 'bluies' (letters) he received from home (see page 51). *(D Notman)*

9. What the well-dressed Royal Scot was wearing. (see pages 54 to 55). Colour Sergeant Speirs in desert combats and chest webbing, complete with L2 grenades, poses by Major Potter's Warrior. *(G Richardson)*

10. The newly elected Prime Minister, John Major, visits The Royal Scots during his tour of 4 Brigade, 8 January, 1991. *(P Fagan)*

11. Angus McLeod marries Tina Fenton at Al Jubail, 20 January, 1991. (*W Smart*)

12. First Aid training. Because of the predictions of high casualties, extra training was given so that every man could save a comrade's life. (*R Walker*)

13. A pintle-mounted Milan anti-tank missile on a 432. Later the Milan Platoon received Warriors. (*E Edwards*)

14. Mortar Platoon 'Bombing-up' a 432. "We got given tons of them, tons and tons and tons and tons of them!" Pte Scott Gillies (see page 66). (*P Fagan*)

15. Captain George Lowder, Adjutant (centre), briefs
Lieutenant-Colonel Iain Johnstone, during one of the large scale
exercises, January,1991. (*The Royal Scots*)

16. The Battle Group assembled for a full scale exercise, January 1991.
(*R Walker*)

17. Jocks of B Company line up to board a transport aircraft for Al Quaysumah, 26 January, 1991. (*R Walker*)

18. B Company Jocks dig-in in the Assembly Area, February, 1991. (*D Notman*)

19. The vehicles of Battle Group Main drawn into a defensive 'Hedgehog', 15 February, 1991. *(R Brindley)*

20. 4 Brigade vehicles practise breaking through the berm. *(G Richardson)*

21. 18 February, 1991, 2nd Lieutenant Roger Walker receives a 'jag' (inoculation) against Saddam Hussein's biological weapons. (*The Royal Scots*)

22. "We have just received the plan, Awesome . . . " Iain Johnstone holds an 'O Group' for his officers, 18 February, 1991 (see page 75). Centre left (kneeling) Major Norman Soutar, O/C A Company and (seated) Major John Potter O/C B Company. (*Mike Moore*)

23. "Right down to the wood!" A Jock has his hair cut just before the start of the ground offensive. Note the desert camouflaged NBC suits and rubber overboots. (*R Walker*)

24. A moment's pause for reflection in the Staging Area, Sunday 24 February, 1991. (*R Brindley*)

I was a rifleman; we sat in the back. You've got your driver, your gunner, your commander. The driver sits in the front and drives [the Warrior], the commander sits in the turret with the gunner. The commander we had was a Sarge [Sergeant].

There are seven men in the back. At one side you have your section commander and he has his LSW [Light Support Weapon] man and his rifleman. On our side we had an LSW, a GPMG [General Purpose Machine-Gun] and two riflemen. One of them was a section Two I/C, officially a Lance Corporal, but we had a Private at the time.

There's a lot of kit in the back of the Warrior, so you don't have a lot of room.

[When the Warrior stopped], one man ran out to one side, to the opposite side he was sitting on, and he got down and the guy opposite him ran round to the other side. You just keep doing [that until the whole section is deployed on the ground]. Sometimes the Warrior just keeps moving as you're doing it. The people in the Warrior, they keep firing all the time. The GPMG is firing all the time.

The guys on the right, they get to move, then they'll fire on that position and the other team gets to move. I was the GPMG No2, I was armed with the SA80 as well, so I carried spare ammo for the GPMG [and a] LAW 80. It's very quick, 'cause when you're there your adrenalin is really pumping.

Private Vincent Stott

Gaining entry to the Iraqi trenches was the job of the Point Section, which was to make and secure an entrance so that the rest of the company could push through and clear the objective.

You debus as the Warrior gives covering fire. You just smack a couple of grenades, just to give an entrance, a couple of grenades to take out anybody that's there and that's where we made our entrance. We were Point Section, that means we're the guys that make the hole, we bust the hole into the trench system. If it's defended we take out the first guys, [and] get in there. That was our job, somebody had to do it.

The rest of the sections, in fact the rest of the Company came through us. One section would come in, take it as far as they could go, next section through them and that's the way it would go on, they just went through each other until they were finished. Hard work when you're doing it, but boring as well, because you've done your bit and you see these people going through you and banging forward.

Private Tom Gow, 5 Platoon, B Company

Sitting in the back of a Warrior, closed down, in full kit, was going to be quite an ordeal for the fighting troops. In addition to the desert combat uniform, each man would be wearing the latest NBC "Noddy" suit[5], a CBA (Combat Body Armour) vest, and full webbing. On the head was worn the new Helmet, Combat GS Mk6, with its resin-bonded ballistic nylon shell and shock-absorbent liner. This was fitted with a desert DPM cover on which was sewn a patch of Hunting Stewart tartan denoting the Royal Scots' Battle Group (on the left side), and a small metal tag (at the back) showing the Company and vehicle call sign of the wearer. In addition, each man had his name, appointment and blood group written, in felt pen, on the helmet cover, CBA and NBC suit.

Standard footwear throughout the Battalion was the black leather high-leg boot. While some of the other units provided themselves with commercially produced sand-coloured suede desert boots, the Royals, conscious of the forthcoming battle, stuck to the issue footwear which would be easier to decontaminate if there was a chemical attack. Canvas- and suede-topped desert boots were eventually issued after the ground war was over, and some of the recipients grumbled that they were too late, but it seems likely that they were intended as a summer issue for the troops on *"roulement"*.

The web equipment on issue to the Royal Scots was the recently introduced 1990 Pattern PLCE (Personal Load

Carrying Equipment). Made from Cordura, a type of nylon webbing, it was similar in some respects to the 1958 Pattern, previously used, in which most of the soldier's fighting load had been carried on the waistbelt.

But this was not an ideal arrangement for armoured infantry who might have to sit for many hours in a Warrior IFV, and the addition of the respirator haversack, containing NBC equipment, on to an already crammed waistbelt was a potential problem for some of the leaner soldiers. It was particularly difficult for vehicle crews to negotiate the cramped access to the turret and driver's seat while wearing their webbing. Lieutenant Chris Brannigan offered a solution. He had seen some of the soldiers on patrol in Northern Ireland wearing privately-purchased commercially-made combat vests, in which the soldiers' immediate needs were carried in pockets on the chest. He contacted Arktis, a manufacturer of web equipment, based in Exeter, who agreed to make a prototype to his design. The finished product, in Cordura printed with a camouflage design, was widely adopted throughout both 4th and 7th Brigades. It consisted of three large ammunition pouches placed centrally on the chest, flanked by two utility pouches which could carry a water-bottle or small items of kit, and two smaller pouches suitable for grenades. Behind the central pouches at the front was a large kangaroo pocket for maps and papers. The equipment was held in place by a broad strap over each shoulder, and a waist strap which fastened at the side. Two small pouches could be slipped on to the shoulder straps to carry a compass, first aid kit or field dressing. There was even a commanders' version in which the outside pouch on the left side was replaced by a pistol holster, and this was carried by some of the Brigade staff.

Although the Royal Scots were allowed to choose which-ever type of webbing they preferred, some opted for the issued 1990 Pattern because the chest webbing raised the wearer off the ground when prone, making him feel more exposed on the flat desert terrain.

I didn't like the chest webbing. It's good for FIBUA, but it's no good [when you are] crawling, because it's always getting in the way, you can't get really down. With the other webbing you can get down.

Private Vincent Stott

The worst bit is keeping the sand out of your magazines. Because it gets into your webbing and if you are doing an exercise, mostly lying down, you get up about two stone heavier with all the sand in your pouches and pockets!

Private Tom Gow

All the men carried one or two "Day" or "Jet" sacks – the side pockets from the '90 Pattern Bergen rucksack – fastened on to a yoke, to carry a spare NBC suit and extra ammunition and, of course, the respirator haversack was carried by everyone, either on the waistbelt or on its own waist strap.

The normal rifleman's load of four magazines of ammunition was doubled, but some of the machine-gunners carried even more.

I had 1800 rounds on me every time I went out on to a position. I had 200 rounds on the front, two belts [of ammunition in] two pouches in the front, it was a roll like a pasta slice. I actually obtained two old '58 pattern water-bottle pouches and put [the ammunition belts into them]. I found the chest webbing that we had out there was a bit of a problem because you had too much weight on your front, and you were keeling. If you were going down, [you] couldnae' get back up. So I [had] 200 on my front, [and] we had two jet sacks and I had 800 [rounds] in each, so that's the way I divided it up on my back.

Private Stuart McDonald, Machine-Gunner, 6 Platoon,
B Company

The 5.56m SA80 automatic rifle was the standard personal weapon throughout the Battalion, and each section had a Light Support Weapon (LSW) which was a heavier version of the SA80 and had been introduced to replace the 7.62mm General Purpose Machine Gun. However, each section also had a GPMG to give it even greater fire-power. Some officers carried 9mm Browning Hi Power Pistols for prisoner-of-war handling, and everyone carried the standard L2 High Explosive and White Phosphorous grenades. A new weapon issued while the Battalion was in training in the Gulf was the Close Light Assault Weapon (CLAW), a rifle grenade which fitted on the barrel of the SA80. It had been in service with the French forces but had not been introduced for service with the British Army up to that time. This weapon bridged the gap between the hand grenade and the light mortar, and was to be particularly useful for reaching inaccessible bunkers or dug-in vehicles.

While the Coalition Forces prepared for war, the deadline of 15 January for the Iraqi withdrawal from Kuwait, imposed under UN Resolution 678, expired unheeded by the Iraqis. The world waited as the countdown to war began.

It was clear that the ground war would be preceded by an air offensive and over 2,000 aircraft, manned by crews from eleven nations, were combat ready and on full alert. At 3am on 17 January (local time) a massive air strike was mounted by the Coalition. One of the first strikes was made by Tornados of the RAF whose job it was to neutralize the Iraqi airforce by low-level attacks on the runways which led from the hardened shelters housing the Iraqi aircraft. The Tornados' principal weapon for this task was the JP233 which dropped a series of explosive devices designed to make the runways not only unusable but also virtually beyond repair. Some of the explosive devices tore up the concrete, and cratered the ground beneath, while others scattered anti-personnel mines over the entire area to deter repair parties. Meanwhile, with almost surgical precision,

US bombers were attacking specific targets in Baghdad in order to disrupt the Iraqi military chain of command and support lines.

The Royal Scots awoke that morning to an NBC alert.

17 January 1991 – D-Day. First *No Duff* Gas attack. Masked up at 0430 hrs, unmasked one hour later.

Lieutenant Guy Richardson

Although this was the first real alert, it proved to be a false alarm, but by this time the Royals had real confidence in their equipment, which was highly sought after by the US members of the Coalition, and they had been given a more rational assessment of the danger from chemical and biological weapons. They were also taking NAPS tablets which are a nerve agent pre-treatment. They can be supplemented at the time of an attack by injection into the soldier's leg with a "Combi-pen".

We were briefed by a doctor at 5 Armoured Field Ambulance, if you take your NAPS tablet, the only way [the Iraqis are] going to kill you with a nerve agent is if they grab you by your ankles and hold you upside down in a bucket [of it]!

We had a hell of a lot of confidence in the British [NBC] Kit.

Private Scott Gillies

An important task, completed just as the Air War started, was the "Up-Armouring" of the vehicles. Drawing on the experience of 7 Brigade, fine filters had been fitted to the engines, but now additional armoured plates were to be bolted on to the Warriors and 432s.

The sections had to up-armour their own vehicles. We were under the instruction of the attached LAD, REME fitters; they drilled the holes where they knew the nuts and bolts had to go, but we had to fit the armour and that took us a long time. It took us all night, a good thirty-six hours anyway, just to up-armour one vehicle. It was a ten-man lift; a whole section just to lift up one piece of armour. That was quite a strenuous night. That actually started the day before the air war started and we just finished it as the air war started. We got a "gas gas gas" [alert] that morning, because they fired the first Scud. Obviously the whole world thought it was heading towards them, so everybody masked up.

Lance Corporal Geoffrey McDermid, 4 Platoon, B Company

On 20 January Captain Angus McLeod, Commander of the Reconnaissance Platoon, married Captain Tina Fenton, an RAMC anaesthetist serving with 33rd Field Hospital. The couple had been engaged for some time, and the bride-to-be had gone out to the Gulf with 7 Brigade. They managed to get permission to marry under a wartime act that had not been used since the Second World War. The wedding was attended by Colonel Johnstone and a representative contingent from the Battalion, including Guy Richardson who was Best Man. The newly-weds had a brief honeymoon in Al Jubayl, but it was rumoured that they spent their wedding night in respirators and full NBC kit because of a Scud alert.

The air war was accompanied by leaflets dropped by the Psychological Operations Team to induce the Iraqis to surrender, and these were avidly sought after as souvenirs by the Coalition troops. But to a non-Arabic reader, the cartoon sketch on the leaflet appeared meaningless. However, a translation of the text, on the reverse of one, was very explicit in its message:

"Soldiers of the Iraqi 12th Armoured Division. The day has come for you to make a decision. Soon the screams of your dying comrades will echo in your ears. You will watch the bodies of many of your brothers shredded by the fierce weapons of an Armoured Division. The decision must now be made. If you stay and fight you will die. If you are wise men and wish to live and see your families again, you will turn your tank turrets around, move away from your tanks and your equipment. Remove the magazine from your weapon. Place the weapon over your left shoulder with the muzzle down and as you approach the advancing tanks, place your hands over your head and proceed slowly. This is the only way you can escape certain death by the overwhelming allied war machine."[6]

Naturally some of the Jocks took great pains to see if it was physically possible to put your hands up while carrying your rifle muzzle downwards over your left shoulder. They concluded that the Iraqis should also be advised to hop on one leg while juggling three oranges as they surrendered, and for a time a common greeting within the Royals' lines was a quick juggling action with the hands while hopping towards each other.

Training for war entails risk. Ensuring that the men were fully capable of undertaking the task in hand was paramount, so peacetime safety standards had to be altered to allow training to progress.

As the training stepped up and the men made the transition from normal range work to trench clearing with live ammunition, so the risk of injury increased. Schemes which might have caused a sharp intake of breath had they been suggested in Germany became normal as the men's confidence and ability increased. It was essential to give the Jocks experience of the type of warfare they were to expect, in as realistic a way as possible, to get them used to "the sights and sounds of battle", and it was just not practical to have the peacetime level of safety personnel in attendance to ensure that no man allowed the muzzle of his weapon to point anywhere other than his allowed arc of fire. Inevitably there were some accidents, but fortunately none of them fatal.

You've got to understand that it was very, *very, very*, realistic training. The boys were fired up. As far as they were concerned this was the real thing. We trained realistically; the Commanding Officer directed us to. Colonel Iain said, "You will train hard and realistically," and that was it; we went for it.

'On Devil Dog Dragoon Range [the individual ranges] had Tango or India names. India, I think for Infantry. India Eight was the range [we were on] and it was a sort of mock Iraqi trench complex. We were taking one of the companies through, I think it was probably A Company, and Steve Telfer and John Gillespie-Payne, both of them, were the wrong side of a grenade.

The Jocks were getting stuck into it and they were shouting, as you should shout, "Grenade", when you chuck a grenade. But the swines were chucking two bloody grenades! So you took cover until the first one went off, then you stood up and the buggers had thrown another one! John Gillespie-Payne was the first casualty and he ended up flat on his back and he was unconscious for a while till we managed to get him up. Then Steve Telfer; I was about five yards, no more than that, behind Steve, just coming out of a trench, and he was standing on the parapet acting as Safety Officer. I just put my head up and saw this L2 grenade; it landed bloody close to him. The thing went off and I thought, "Well that's the end of Telfer. All I'll see is a pair of steaming boots!" But he sort of picked himself off the ground, shouted, "Bastard!" and dusted the sand off himself and then he and his signaller, Private Clark, just picked little bits of shrapnel out of their arms and carried on. They were very lucky they didn't get a base plate or anything through them, just tiny bits of coiled wire.

Major Kirk Gillies

On 18 January a night attack on Devil Dog Dragoon Range resulted in a more serious accident. Major Bryan Johnston, Commander of Fire Support Company, was acting as Safety Officer when he was shot in the arm and stomach while A Company was making its way through the trenches.

It was just about that time that O/C Fire Support Company was shot by accident on one of the hill firing ranges. My Company was waiting to go on next and we were really more concerned with getting him out of the way so that we could carry on training than if he lived or died actually. It was like that, just get the helicopter in and get him out of there so we can crack on. Then we realized that our attitudes had hardened to such a point that preparation for the war or training was paramount and nothing would be allowed to get in the way of it. By that stage we were absolutely committed to going all out for it.

Major John Potter

Everything was dark; it was a run through one of the Iraqi [style] trenches. There was a lot of overhead fire, everyone was firing, it was all live rounds, and it was pitch black, [you] couldn't see a thing. We were firing away and we heard this screaming, and then someone shoved up some mini flares and some Shermulies[7], [then] you could see everything, it was like daytime. You could see him and you heard him screaming. A medic waggon came along and they had to deal with it.

Private Vincent Stott

Guy Richardson was among the first on the scene and administered first aid, binding up his company commander's wounds with field dressings and giving him a shot of morphine.[8]

I was about fifty metres off to his right and there were wooden targets there, bunkers there and so on. Someone must have identified him as a target. Simple as that, and he was shot.

He was wearing a flak jacket which undoubtedly saved his life, no question about it. I think a total of two or three rounds hit him. The most damaging one went into his side and actually lodged in his buttock. We didn't realize this at the time. I remember turning to my left and seeing him going down screaming. There was a checkfire on everything. [I] ran across, we administered first aid; gave him morphine and so on, patched him up. We found one entry wound but we couldn't find an exit wound, so we had to keep looking for the exit wound, make sure we'd covered all parts of his body because a bullet can go in one, and go out of a completely different area. And we just simply couldn't find the exit wound.

We got him patched up, we took him to an ambulance, and there was quite a wait whilst the helicopter came. I was sitting there making sure he was OK and he kept on saying, "My arm,

62

my arm!", and I'd looked at his arm. I said, "Where on your arm?" He said, "Just here", and I looked at it and it seemed to be OK. I just couldn't see anything, and eventually he said, "No, its further up, further up". So I got a pair of scissors and cut up and I rolled back his sleeve and a ricochet, it was obviously a ricocheting bullet, had hit the [upper] part of his arm and there was a very clean half-moon missing. He said, "Is there anything there?", and I turned around and said, "No it's only a graze, Bryan; you'll be all right." So I put another field dressing over it and didn't obviously tell him.

The funny thing [was], all the time Bryan was carrying a dictaphone around with him and as this was all happening in the ambulance, he was talking into the dictaphone, he was talking to his wife. High on the morphine so he didn't know what was happening, he was [saying] "I'm not sure I'm going to make it." But he was in a great deal of pain.

Eventually the helicopter came, [we] put him in the helicopter, went back to the game and the Commanding Officer stood up and said, "Right we'll get the next Company through!" People were going, "Phew, well one of the safety staff just got shot!", and the Commanding Officer said, "Right, I'm one of the safety staff", leading from example, and everybody's hands went up, "I'll be safety staff", and off [they] went and did the same thing; did another attack.

Lieutenant Guy Richardson

The bullet that entered Bryan Johnston's stomach had hit his flak jacket first and started a downward spiral motion during which it emerged at the lower edge of the armour and ploughed into his abdomen, just below the jacket. It eventually lodged in his buttock, miraculously missing bones and arteries on the way.

Bryan Johnston's life was saved by his CBA (Combat Body Armour), which gave the troops confidence in this, their latest encumbrance.

Up to that point it [the CBA] was seen as a bloody hindrance. It was another bit of bloody kit to wear and even in the turret we thought, "I'm not going to wear this bugger when I go into battle", and after that you thought, "By Christ, I'm going to ensure I keep it on. It guards your vital organs!"

Lieutenant Chris Brannigan, Warrior Captain, A Company

The general opinion of the purpose served by the CBA among the Jocks, however, was that it kept your body together if you were hit by a high velocity round. Fortunately this was never really put to the test.

If I had one contribution I made to the whole campaign it was that when I got shot they knew it was for real, because I was casevac-ed through the normal chain as anticipated and they continued. This was a rehearsal; this could have been the last opportunity they had to do this before crossing the startline. It was the last chance to make any mistakes.

The general feeling was that it was damned dangerous and it was just a matter of time before someone got injured. That afternoon we sat and had some supper beforehand and a butterfly came and landed on me, which we all joked about, "All Quiet on the Western Front" etc, and I was shooing it away.

Last light came, we had the final briefing and I remember one of the plans that was going to be done by one of the companies was that they were going to swing out to the flank, and quite frankly it would have meant that they would end up firing at each other. So we said "No, we can't do that," and I'm not convinced that the message that they couldn't do that actually got down to the ground, because they went on to do it.

We then started the move forward. My Colour Sergeant was complaining he hadn't got any body armour, so I said get it off the driver of one of the Warriors. However, when the Warriors had stopped he went and asked and the driver had already given [away] his body armour. There was a lot of it about, all the important people had it, but my Colour Sergeant for instance, didn't require to have it at that stage. So I said to him. "Have mine", and I ripped it open and this draught of really cold air shot round my waist. It was a bitterly cold night, real Baltic weather, so I said, "Bugger that!" zipped it back up again and said, "You stay with the Warrior; don't bother coming with us. We can cope without you."

Off we went and the first trench position was taken out really well, but then of course, it's almost inevitable that that was the simple one. Then the second wave went in and each time I kept going with the front wave so that when it finished I would be at the end there. The third one, there was a lot of hard open ground to take, actual bunkers, and this is where, as we were going forward, the Jocks just made the bunker and I noticed there was an extraordinary frenzy of fire at my feet as if a whole fire team were firing at the bunker so I shouted "Stop!" and then it was like a Sam Pekinpah movie. I remember getting swung back [hit] in my arm; it swung my body round and then I had this punch in the chest because I'd been turned. It hit me in the stomach, and I went down on to the deck and I remember shouting "Help!" or something. I had my ear-defenders on and my helmet, and everything around me was quiet; that slow-motion followed by complete silence, with this extraordinary pain. I was lying there thinking I've been hit, because of this extraordinary pain in my leg, and my stomach. My first reaction is that's one of my leg's gone. I couldn't really move, and I was lying in a pile.

Major Bryan Johnston

Badly shaken and under the effects of morphine, Bryan Johnston was naturally concerned as to the seriousness of his wound, but his spirits were raised by the Jocks who offered to check the "family jewels" for damage and to look after "yon heavy wallet" which might delay his evacuation. It has even been suggested that someone in A Company ran a book on who it was fired the shots; however, it was clearly an accident so no charges were made.

We trained incredibly hard. I remember at Sennelager not being a hundred percent convinced. Not in the soldiers but in myself. If I was worried about anything, I was worried that I would let the soldiers down because I would make a mess of something, and the biggest fear of anyone in command is that if you make a mess it could well cost people their lives.

[During training] we put in a daytime attack and it was all guns blazing, and I remember thinking my fieldcraft had improved dramatically; that everything in the platoon clicked; they knew what they were going to do; we knew where we were going; we knew the drills within the different vehicles and the sections on the ground all married up.

We put this attack in and it was all live firing and I thought, "This probably [would have] worked!" We were on a bit of a high and, as soon as it was finished, I turned round to one of the Safety Staff and said, "That would have worked, wouldn't it?" He said, "Yes, a couple of points, but the bottom line is it would have worked." For me personally, when that attack went in, I thought, "I'm happy that we can dismount. We can do it."

Lieutenant Colin Dougan

Over the next few days Battle Group manoeuvres continued and every man was issued with a second set of desert combat uniform. Practice in breaching the expected defensive berm followed during the next two days and just before the move north-west the Battle Group "bombed-up" all its vehicles with as much ammunition as they could carry in preparation for the ground war.

There's less space in a Mortar 432 than there is in a Warrior because of the amount of ammunition we carry. A hundred and sixty-four rounds we carry, mainly HE and Smoke, some Illum [Illuminating rounds]. We got a lot of boxes strapped to the outside for personal kit. It didn't look like an armoured vehicle by the time we had finished, it looked like a gypsy caravan. There was bits hanging off everywhere.

One day we'd been sitting there and we got told right, here come some vehicles with ammo; unload all your HE and we got given the new proxi [proximity] rounds, and we got given tons of them, tons and tons and tons and tons of them!

[The ammunition] comes ready assembled, but you've got to condition it before you put it into the vehicles; take all the packing off.

[We loaded] them into the vehicles and then we just looked and we'd piles left; growing everywhere! We just had to load them up as best as possible, they were underneath seats, strapped to the side, strapped to the roof, strapped to the back. Thinking back on it now, if we'd been hit they'd still be looking for parts of us!

Private Scott Gillies

On 24 January the 1st (British) Armoured Division began Exercise Dibdabah Drive, the first phase of the move into position for the start of the ground offensive. At last the Royals were on their way to war. On 25 January the armoured vehicles were loaded on to transporters to be driven to Concentration Area KEYES overnight, and the next morning the men would be flown forward to Al Qasumah airstrip to reunite with them.

The "B" vehicles (non-armoured, wheeled vehicles) were to be driven by their crews in convoy also to rendezvous with the Battle Group before the breakthrough into Iraq. Before they departed, in case there was not another opportunity, the Colonel gave the order to knock out all vehicle windscreens. It would make them less easy to spot as they would no longer reflect the bright sunlight, and it would be safer for the crews if they came under fire. The drivers were issued with commercially-produced ski-goggles to protect their eyes while they were driving.

As the freshly unglazed convoy got under way and the former inhabitants of the armoured vehicles settled down for their first night without shelter, the heavens opened and the rain poured down!

The night the vehicles moved, I said, "Right lads, we'll take minimum kit here. Take your sleeping bags, take your bivvy bags and whatever." My bivvy bag was packed away 'cause I'd never used it. Away we went and we sat outside [on] this road and then the rain came, didn't it! And it hammered down. That's the only night I never took my bivvy bag, it hammered down. Kept me awake, and kept me fresh!

Corporal Derek Notman

I was on the convoy that night. We'd lost all our windscreens; it was a cold wet night, and we were almost late getting to the convoy, because we'd been going to the local garage and getting chocolate bars and so on, and it was about a ten-mile drive. We were rushing down there with hundreds of pounds of chocolates, and then eventually we arrived at the convoy in time, and it was a really slow start. Eight o'clock we had to report and we didn't go through with the convoy until midnight. We shunted forward a bit and waited and we arrived at the start of the convoy release point and I was following the guy in front because that's what convoy driving's all about. But the light changed to red and the vehicle in front disappeared and this guy said, "Stop!" I said, "I can't. I'm following that vehicle." He said, "Stop, you are the first of the next package." I had never been in an Army convoy in my life and I said, "I'm the Padre." He said, "Report to that tent". There was this Captain sitting there, and I said, "Look something's gone wrong here with this package. I don't know where I'm going. I haven't got a map." He said, "You don't need a map. You've got three minutes before you start. There isn't time to do anything else. This is what you do: you drive at 20 ks an hour and off you go!"

So I got back in the vehicle and I said to Butch [the driver], "We're leading this package but don't worry, there's no problem; just drive at 20 ks we'll be fine." And he said, "The speedo's bust!"

Major Stephen Blakey

My vehicle was taken off us. The driver went up with it; we all went to the airhead. I was all right. I had my sleeping bag and my bivvy bag with me; a lot of the guys were caught out.

Most of the guys got put on a Hercules. We were sitting there, wondering what we'll get; then in flies a Chinook [helicopter]. A Chinook [has] a capacity of about fifty fully loaded men. They managed to squeeze about seventy-four guys on to the Chinook, to fly it up country. They had guys sitting on the floor and everything, bergens and rifles and webbing and sleeping bags.

[We arrived in] Area KEYES and it was Burns night, 'cause they'd managed to fly out some Haggis to us. We never had any turnip, but we had potatoes, so everything was fine and dandy then.

Private Scott Gillies

At the end of January elements of the Iraqi 5th Mechanized Division crossed the Kuwait/Saudi border and occupied the abandoned oil processing town of Al Khafji. Only 8 miles south of the Kuwait border, the town was within Iraqi artillery range and had been bombarded on the first night of the air war. The 20,000 inhabitants had consequently been evacuated because it was impossible to defend.

A Saudi Arabian tank battalion was despatched to cut off the northern route into the town, while Qatari units, supported by US Marines, moved into place to prevent any further advance. The Saudi force soon discovered that it was outnumbered by the remainder of the Iraqi 5th Division lined up on the road into town, so wisely withdrew. Meanwhile the British 4 Brigade, also close to the border, was alerted.

There was one time when we were doing exercises we got an hour to move, and everyone ran back to the waggon, asking why, what was going on? They were saying the satellite dish had lost a [Iraqi] Division. Then they found it again; they said it was heading towards the border of Saudi Arabia, and at first we were very cocky about it.

"They're actually coming towards us now, after all the bombardments," and that's when we started to panic and think, "Oh God, they're going to attack us!" because the attacker has always got a better side than the defence. But of course they never came through; they actually attacked another wee town in Saudi Arabia, Khafji. I think that's when everybody started getting a wee bit scared, because they were being cocky with it.

Private Stuart McDonald

Without air cover, the Iraqi column was a sitting target for a Coalition air strike. Soon the force in Al Khafji was cut off. The Coalition air forces controlled the northern route, and the ground forces had encircled to the south. Supported by US artillery and aircraft, an Arab force composed of Saudi Arabian and Qatari troops drove the enemy out of town. The Iraqi Division was estimated to have suffered some 800 casualties and only 20% were thought to have escaped.

Exactly what they stood to achieve by this incursion was not clear. At best it was a propaganda stunt, but the media made much of the fact that Iraqi troops could apparently walk into Saudi Arabia and occupy a town unopposed, which understandably infuriated King Fahd. However, the military commanders regarded it as a reconnaissance in force which not only cost the Iraqis nearly a whole division, but furnished the Coalition with some important information. The air supremacy that had almost been achieved would clearly enable a numerically inferior force to engage the Iraqis on the ground and win, and additionally the Iraqi artillery used on this occasion was ineffective because it was inaccurate.

By probing the border to see what reaction it would provoke, Saddam Hussein's army had revealed much about its own inadequacy which bode well for the Coalition forces in the coming "Mother of all Battles". Every piece of information was evaluated and passed through the chain of command to keep the ground forces up to date.

In the evening [I would] write an Intelligence Report that would be typed up overnight and fired out to the Companies first thing in the morning. They'd have a daily Intelligence Report, established information and the best guess as to what that actually meant, and what implications it might have.

Things got quite exciting around Khafji, because we identified a strange up-armour on the T55s that we'd never seen before. They'd also apparently erected mesh screens in front of the dug-out tank positions which would affect the Milan Anti-Tank weapon. It would go off and hit the screen rather than the tank, and this was just basically a lump of chicken wire, strung in front of it, and burning barrels beside the tank as heat decoys.[9]

When I could I'd go round the Companies and speak; the Jocks had a great thirst for information. You can push things out on paper, but [in their eyes] it was the written word coming from the Platoon Commander who they saw every day. Whereas if the Battalion Intelligence Officer came round it wasn't the same thing, it carried that bit more "street cred" in the Jocks' mind. So when I could I went round, but shuttling forward to Brigade and back, beating your head against the wall for an hour, coming back, getting the papers there ready then going back out again, you didn't have that much time.

Captain Dermot Fulton

Keeping the Jocks properly briefed even meant contradicting some of the newspaper reports that they had read.

One particular comment in a Scottish newspaper likened the Republican Guard to the SAS. Britain's elite force are the SAS; therefore, if the Republican Guard are Iraq's elite force they must be the equivalent of the SAS. So the Jocks believed that the Iraqis had a hundred and twenty thousand armoured SAS troops. How the hell can you defeat that? But the fact of the matter was they were only elite compared with their normal troops.

The ordinary Iraqi troops were of no quality, and the Republican Guard were only of good quality compared with them. So I tried to convince my guys that the Republican Guard, although they were Iraq's elite, were no better than the standard average Russian soldier.

Unfortunately, because of this one article in the *Daily Record*, I think it was, which is a paper they all read and have faith in, they took a bit of convincing. That one article did a lot of damage.

2nd Lieutenant Roger Walker

On 10 February a Church parade was held at Battle Group Main. This was to be the Royals' last service before crossing into Iraq.

We had a number of last services. That was one of the difficult things about it. Every time we deployed further north or north-west, we didn't know what was going to happen at the next location and whether we would be able to hold services.

I suppose my major theme through the whole thing was that while I would like to say, "God is on our side and if you pray to God you'll live, he will protect you", I don't believe that is what the Gospel is about. But what I do believe it's about is, God has promised to be with those who draw close to Him. That God would be with us whatever happened, and we should go and do the job that we have been given to do by our country. That He promises to be with us. If we choose to allow Him into our lives, He'll be with us and give us the strength and the support and the presence we need, whatever happens to us. That was the essence, really, of what I said all the way through, in different ways, shapes and forms.

It would have been much more comfortable to say, "We're the goodies and they're the baddies, and of course God is on our side," but I don't believe that is realistic. I compared Saddam Hussein to a schoolyard bully who had been behaving in an unacceptable way and had been warned that he must stop or he would be beaten up, as it were, and had chosen not to stop and therefore had to be disciplined. So there was a certain amount of that kind of preaching.

Major Stephen Blakey

Following the visit from the Divisional Commander, General Rupert Smith, the Battle Group prepared itself for Exercise Dibdibah Charge, another massive FTX (Field Training Exercise) during which the whole 1st (British) Armoured Division would move to Assembly Area RAY, about 40 kilometres south of the Saudi/Iraq border and would practise passing through the 1st (US) Mechanized Infantry Division and transiting the breach. All the training that the Battle Group had put in, practising platoon, company and battle group manoeuvres, completely closed down and making minimal use of the communications systems was about to be put to the test.

There's a big difference between the way we used to train in BATUS [in Canada] and in Germany and the way you do it [for real]. The difference between having your head out of the turret, where you can see, all-round vision, and being battened down looking through a sight and a couple of little peep holes in the side, is just incredible, and that's what led to many accidents at the start, many "brushes". We made our errors in training, which was the place to make them.

On various moves, my platoon was spread out in an extended line, with the rest of the Company behind me, including the O/C, and the O/C would sit just behind me. Now he had SATNAV, and I didn't. He knew where he wanted to go, and I didn't, and he would tell me to do things and my platoon would just roll off thataway, and I'd get "Three zero, three zero, you are going the wrong way!" You couldn't speak to your individual callsigns [vehicles] because then you'd start cluttering up the net, and the most important thing we had the net for was for him to command the company. If I needed to command individual callsigns we were just never going to get anywhere. I imagine he was getting it from the CO on the other net in one ear [and] he was giving it to me on his own net.

It worked in the end; it was quite simple; the drills were absolutely simple; it was just performing forms, or fairly large turns unexpectedly. Sometimes I think it was a case of not knowing quite how far to turn. As you wheel through one vehicle, your outside vehicle is having to sort of force itself round there and the inside vehicle is marking time. If it doesn't mark time slowly enough, then it's really difficult to get [the whole platoon] round.

Lieutenant Colin Dougan

In the event, for the Royal Scots Battle Group, this "passage of lines" was turned into utter chaos, with units cutting directly in front of each other.

We practised the conduct of the breach. We had walk-throughs, talk-throughs and then drove through it at night, and it was a complete and utter shambles. I couldn't believe it. The American guides got lost, we ended up in the middle of the breach trying to cut crossways as virtually a whole Corps were coming the other way. It was a nightmare and we thought, If this is what it was going to be like on the day, well it just didn't bear thinking about. As it turned out, through lessons learned that night, when we actually came to do the real thing it was beautiful. Nothing went wrong. But I'd rather it happened that way than went terribly well on the exercise then when we're actually at war there's a fuck up.

Major John Potter

While the Battle Group was rehearsing for the entry into Iraq, the Padre was ensuring that the soldiers could get their Valentine's Day cards home in time.

The NAAFI were selling Valentine cards. We bought hundreds and hundreds of Valentine cards and we got the lads to fill them all in. We didn't charge them postage for it, we sent them back in official mail – broke all the rules – to our families officer back in Werl who put them into the post block, where the wives picked up their mail on St Valentine's Day.

Major Stephen Blakey

On 16 February there was some startling news. It seemed as though Saddam Hussein would agree to withdraw his troops from Kuwait in accordance with a Soviet peace initiative, but the conditions had to be agreed. The United States rejected the plan as falling well short of what was required, so it seemed unlikely to succeed. In the meantime the Jocks had their own ideas about the conditions demanded by Saddam Hussein, which were thought to include 675 virgins, a year's supply of tomatoes and 155 Cruise Missiles!

Two days later, on the 18th, the men received another inoculation, this time against plague, one of the biological weapons Saddam Hussein was thought to have in his arsenal. The same day, at last, the plan devised by General Schwarzkopf was revealed to the ground forces:

18 February 1991: Had to come away early for a CO O'Gp. G-
Day still not known but big "Plan" given to me – Absolutely
Awesome!!

Lieutenant Guy Richardson

I remember hearing an old World War Two Chaplain talking
about his role as being the "Joker in the Pack". I thought, "Load
of nonsense. He's a man of God, what's he talking about?" I just
couldn't understand what he was talking about at all. But subcon-
sciously I drifted into actually fulfilling that kind of role, and I
would do silly things at O Groups sometimes.

It wasn't necessarily the final O Group, but the big one where
all the really big orders were given out for going through the
breach and so on. It was long and complicated and quite impressive and at the end the Commander [asked], "Any questions?"
And they came to me and I said something like, "I have no
questions. I didn't understand a word you were talking about!"
and the place just collapsed in fits of laughter. Now I did actually
understand and they knew I understood a lot, but it took the heat
off, took the pressure off.

Major Stephen Blakey

Although the actual date of the start of the ground war was
still not revealed, it was very much on the cards that 4
Brigade, with its high infantry content, would make a
fighting crossing of the breach into Iraq, and the Royal
Scots Battle Group had been given a large Iraqi position,
code-named BRASS[10], as its first objective. An aerial
reconnaissance had been carried out and the resulting photographic jigsaw was given to the Battle Group Intelligence
staff.

We had BRASS very well worked out, [from] an aerial photography
run. The accuracy of photographs – they'd given us an infra-red
scan of where positions were but it wasn't to scale and it wasn't
focusing. Reg Brindley who was our Forward Air Controller, he's
actually a qualified Navigator, and Colour Sergeant Lusty, who
was the Assistant IO [Intelligence Officer] actually spent four or

five hours plotting this on to a map. It was remarkable how accurate that turned out to be. Within metres, that is how accurate they'd been, considering the information they had to work from. The plane hadn't been flying a level flight so they had different perspectives, different angles, during the whole flight, so it was a bit of a nightmare job. Well that was [done by those] two guys sitting in the back of the APC Crucible, which was the Battalion Main HQ, with Tilley lamps, people wandering around them, engines revving up. [They were] pretty tired anyway, and they just had a slide rule, a compass and all the rest of it, so it was a major feat. I think the CO based all his plans on that, certainly the direction we came in from.

Captain Dermot Fulton

Thursday, 21 February, 1991: CO called myself and C Sgt Lusty into the Int [Intelligence] wagon to look at some imagery from an F-4. Spent from 2000 to 0115 preparing a map from the unevenly expanding imagery. C Sgt Lusty kept me awake with coffee and kept the flow of good ideas coming as my brain "seized" at times. Bed 0120. Absolutely whacked.

Flight Lieutenant Reg A. Brindley RAF, Forward Air Controller

The news that there would be no Iraqi withdrawal came on 21 February, although by this time there can be few who seriously thought it was still a possibility.

On 24 February, "G-Day", the ground war started. Iraqi shore defences were bombarded by US Naval vessels off the coast of Kuwait, and landing craft were launched to continue the deception that an amphibious assault was about to take place. Meanwhile a mock assault was made on the Wadi Al Batin. These served to divert the Iraqis' attention from an assault along the coast towards Kuwait City by Arab Coalition forces and US Marines, and a blocking move by the US XVIII Corps, including the French force, far to the west which was to cut off southern Iraq and Kuwait. The next day, the main attack by the US VII Corps, including the British 1st Armoured Division, would be launched.

A Singleness of Purpose

The British force's task was to protect the southern flank of the US Corps' advance, then to swing northwards with the Americans to take on the Iraqi Republican Guard.

In their waggons and under their camouflaged nets the Royals made their final preparations.

Any man that says he wasn't scared is a liar! The worst part was writing the last letter. I wrote to my fiancee.

Private Scott Gillies

We got told a couple of days before that we were going in and everyone was getting psyched up, everyone's adrenalin was pumping. You were just sitting in the back [of the Warrior] with all your kit. It was a tight squeeze, sitting down for hours on end. You had everything on, you had your desert suit on, your NBC suit on, NBC boots, and you had your webbing on, and your rifle strapped to you.

Private Vincent Stott

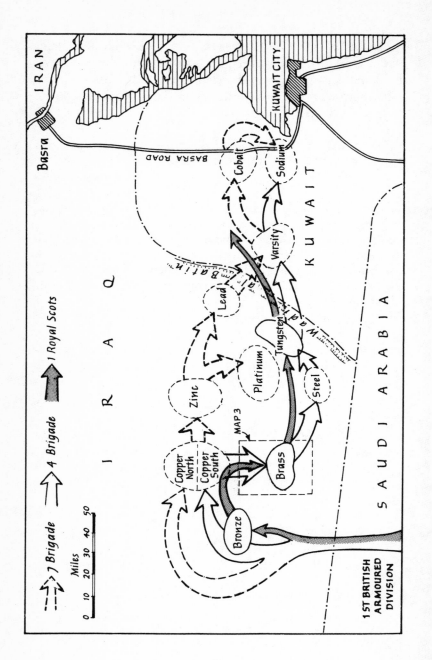

Chapter 3

SHOCKED!

*If you've just been hit by all the preceding artillery, and
suddenly then you get 30 tonnes worth of Warrior haring
through the middle of the night at you, then you're
shocked!*

Lieutenant Alastair Stobie

OBJECTIVE BRONZE

At last the waiting was almost over. The Battle Group
formed up in the Staging Area before receiving the order to
move through the breach and into Iraq.

We went from 60m NTM [notice to move] → immediate & then
moved up into Staging Area. Where I write this. "Booby Traps"
seem to be the thing & so people must stay clear of all kit!!
Tomorrow 1 UK Div, all going well will take over the battle from
1 US Div. The "evening before battle" feels like a night before a
big rugby game – strange that!! Everything aside I'm glad the wait
is over and I feel no remorse for the Iraqis whatsoever. Up the
Royals! Masked up for [about] 20 mins – False alarm.

Lieutenant Guy Richardson

Mid-afternoon on 25 February the Battle Group entered the
breach. The hatches on the vehicles were closed down and
everyone was in full NBC protective equipment, less gloves
and respirator. This surely would be when the Iraqis

unleashed their chemical weapons. The US advance had been very swift, but were the Iraqis setting a trap? They had a known tactic of folding in the middle and then enveloping the attacker. What had become of the Iraqi air force[1]? Were the aircraft being kept for a massive air strike? Did the estimates of the "attrition" of the Iraqi ground forces apply to their capacity to deliver chemical-filled artillery shells?

I think we were a bit scared about the breach because we'd been told [we would] almost certainly come under chemical attack [going] through. Originally we were going to have a hell of a fight getting over, but it did not turn out that way. I think we got through quite easily. We actually got through the breach a lot quicker than they anticipated. You knew you were going through because you could feel [it]. Normally it was sand, really flat for miles and miles and miles, just like driving on the roads, and you'd get a rare speed out of the Warriors. Suddenly it starts getting all bumpy, but the DVC up the top there he was telling us what happened, the breach was massive and all that.

The OC came up on the net, "I hope you've all got your passports stamped; we've now just entered Iraq", that was us away. We shook out when we got over and the DVC started to describe all the positions that had been there, that had been taken out by the air strikes the weeks previous. We expected heavy artillery attacks and chemical agent attacks. Hopefully it wouldn't have slowed us down, but that's what we were expecting. It was a good feeling once you were back on the hard sand again, speeding away again, rather than going through very slowly.

Corporal Derek Notman

I was scared; I think everybody was scared. In the back of the waggon everybody kept quiet all the way through.

Private Kevin Newton, 5 Platoon, B Company

Going through was a bit of an anti-climax really; you looked out and you could see what was going on around you. The Americans had literally bulldozed it flat; there weren't the trenches; the vehicles that were there were three-quarters buried and when you saw the top half of a T55 that was just peeled apart, destroyed, it was a really good feeling to know that someone previous to you had the firepower to do it. It is a great weight off your mind to know that they got through with so little problem.

Lieutenant Alastair Stobie

Although there were strict instructions that all vehicles were to be closed down, some men opened the hatches or the rear doors a fraction to catch a glimpse of the breach as they entered Iraq. This could be justified to a degree for it was thought that a direct hit on the vehicle, even if it did not penetrate the armour, could set up a shock wave that would kill all the occupants unless the air pressure had some avenue of escape. The "over-pressure" from the air filtration system which was designed to prevent any chemical agents from entering, would still work even if the vehicle was not completely closed down.

The move through the breach itself, it was a lot shorter than most people expected. During the practice [it lasted] a few hours, but the actual thing only lasted an hour or so, the move through. We should have been closed down, but the guys in the back had the door open taking their happy snaps.

Lance Corporal Geoffrey McDermid

In the back of the Warriors the tension built up; for many of the soldiers this was when they felt most vulnerable. In one waggon tempers flared and, although the men had expected to fight their way through the breach, a different sort of fight occurred.

Everybody was a bit tight, one guy got right anti – I don't know if he got scared or whatever, but he was – you could see he got a bit tight, and we came to blows, had a couple of wee scuffles as we were going along.

Private Paul Hosie, 6 Platoon, B Company

While the Royal Scots Battle Group was on its way to the Forming Up Position (FUP), just across the border in Iraq, the Commanding Officer received a call from Brigade changing the plan. They would not be moving straight in to attack BRASS, the task they had been briefed for. Instead an Iraqi artillery position codenamed BRONZE, which was originally to have been dealt with by the Royal Fusiliers, was now the Royal Scots' first objective.

We transited forward to the FUP which is where we shook out into our assault formation and awaited the final order to go. On the way to the FUP the Brigade Commander changed the plan. This was slightly disconcerting; we were suddenly told to attack a position that had been earmarked for 3RRF and so as a result in the original orders I hadn't taken much attention to it.

Radio communication was very bad[2] so it took about an hour and a half to get this, the order, through. I then had the problem of trying to contact my own company commanders and, although I got the gist of it through, I decided to call them in for orders when we arrived at the FUP.

So once we got there and the vehicles were filling up by jerry can which we carried with us, the company commanders came to me for orders. There were bomblets[3] around and, we believed, some mines, so they were sort of hopping in amongst the tracks. It started to rain. There was an FAC [Forward Air Control] vehicle, from 7 Brigade, which had broken down beside mine and all its radio sets were interfering with mine and so things were going a little bit down hill. But I gave them the orders very quickly [and] we had something to eat.

Lt.Colonel Iain Johnstone

At this stage the 1st (British) Armoured Division was within Iraqi artillery range, assuming of course that the Iraqis, who had no aerial reconnaissance and probably no means of communicating between formations, could discover where the Division was. Still, the potential threat remained. It had also been decided that the area was to be used as a divisional logistical site and therefore had to be cleared, so an assault was to be launched on BRONZE.

The orders were hurriedly relayed through the chain of command as time was pressing and it was necessary to form up and cross the Start Line at 8pm.

Meanwhile, close on the heels of an airstrike by the Americans' A10 aircraft, the Royal Artillery were pounding the Iraqi position with MLRS (Multi-Launch Rocket System).

So it came over the [radio] net, "Go to your platoon commander's waggons, and walk in the tracks [of the vehicles]. Don't walk anywhere else, because of the danger of the bomblets." So off we went up to the platoon commander's waggon and we were told we were taking out a brigade-sized artillery position, something like that. It sort of hit you then, this was *you*, going in *there*.

It was a hell of a night, it was just teeming down with rain, it was cold and just as I left the platoon commander's waggon to go back to my own, that was when the MLRS – the Multi-Launch Rocket System – went off. At night time. I've never seen anything like it in my life, and I'm never ever likely to forget it either. It was when I was walking back to my waggon, seeing all this going off. We'd got this and I felt sorry for the poor sods on the other side.

Corporal Billy Paul, 2 Platoon, A Company

Not everyone realized that this tremendous fire-power was directed onto the Iraqis by the Royal Artillery, however.

Now at that stage we were all a bit jumpy. We'd just come through the breach into a holding area when the artillery went off. None of us knew whether it was [ours or theirs] or what it was and there was great duck for cover. I poked my head out gingerly afterwards and thought "Christ, that was actually ours!" I went down to the back of the waggon and said to Norman [Soutar], "Ours or theirs?" He said, "I think it was ours."

We had a Sony boogie box, a cassette recorder which we took out and Norman had an opera tape, and he played this tape and

I've never seen such a calming effect on people and I said, "Hmm, that's what they call practical leadership!"

Lieutenant Chris Brannigan

In training previously we used to get thrown about the training fields in Soltau in Germany and "O Groups" [Orders Groups] would be very short and we'd say, "Och, in real life you'd get much longer than that to prepare your orders, if this was a real war!" Matter of fact, when it came we had seconds.

There were no orders really. Norman [Soutar] said, "Look guys, the Brigadier has changed the plan. We've got to go to objective BRONZE", and he gave the suspected layout of the enemy there. Bang! Off went the MLRS, "That's hitting BRONZE now; back to your waggons; we roll in five minutes."

And in that five minutes I took out an American MRE ration pack and offered one of these to the boys. Some didn't want it and some did. But I didn't feel like eating. I sat in and ate the whole thing to try and instil a feeling of calm and normality about life, and say, "Hell, this is the Royal Scots, this is what we are about. Let's crack on and get the business done!"

Captain Robert Bruce

Some of the soldiers paused to reflect on what they were about to do.

I was listening to a personal stereo myself; the rest of the guys were sitting down on one side of the vehicle having a chat and somebody had brought a bottle of whisky, we weren't supposed to have, but they'd kept it for a toast before we went in, so we all had a toast. Then everybody had their own thoughts for five or ten minutes. I was listening to that Harps song, *Alone* it was called. It just happened to be on the tape at that time, but when I was listening it started to sink in what was going to happen.

We were going to move off, but there was a delay. I was sitting there and it started to sink in. Everybody just took five or ten minutes on their own.

That morning in fact our section commander lost his wedding ring. He had it round his neck on a chain, and he lost it that

25. CO's O Group in Staging Area 4, just before mounting up to cross into Iraq. Major John Potter (foreground left), Lieutenant Colonel Iain Johnstone (centre) and Captain Andrew Burnett, Commander of the Mortar Platoon (far right). *(G Richardson)*

26. A Warrior of the Anti-Tank Platoon, with a pintle-mounted Milan anti-tank missile, ploughs through the desert sand. *(The Royal Scots)*

27. Entering Iraq on route 'November', 25 February, 1991. (*G Richardson*)

28. The Battle Group's B (non-armoured) vehicles follow a US Guide through the breach, 25 February, 1991. (*W Smart*)

29. Clearing up on Objective BRONZE, early on the morning of 26 February 1991. (see page 96) *(Mike Moore)*

30. Captain Dermot Fulton, the Battalion Intelligence Officer, interrogates a prisoner. *(The Royal Scots)*

31. Private Mark Morrice by his waggon. He and his co-driver took prisoners while they were on a mail run. (see pages 118-120). *(M Morrice)*

32. Lieutenant Wendy Smart, the only woman to serve with The Royal Scots' Battle Group, somewhere in Southern Iraq, 26 February, 1991. (see page 117). *(W Smart)*

morning, and he was in tears, and the whole platoon was out looking for it. But we couldn't find it; he was really upset about that; it was just wee things like that got to everyone you know; it was just the smallest thing upset you. I tried not to think too much about family and home and that, but at that point, that five or ten minutes, it was really all I could think about.

Lance Corporal Geoffrey McDermid

The Battle Group's tactics and Standard Operating Procedures (SOP) were so well practised by now that all that was needed was the route, the location of their objective and the time they were to hit it. The lead elements would be the tanks to deal with any Iraqi armour. B Company would quickly follow up, while A Company watched the flanks and prepared to echelon[4] through to take the next position.

Each vehicle showed a red light at the back as an identification feature. That and the lack of ambient light effectively obscured the Image Intensification sights[5] and made them useless. The Thermal Imaging sights[6] on Challenger which identify heat sources worked fine but they couldn't see the red lights. So despite the ability of Warrior to match Challenger's cross-country speed, the different sighting systems on that night reintroduced the old divide between Infantry and Tanks.

H hour arrived. I counted the Battle Group down. We were expecting to be gassed. We were primed to take up to 100 casualties. We should have been frightened and perhaps we were. As we moved off I offered up a prayer. Please God don't let my vehicle break down again, and we were off.

Lt.Colonel Iain Johnstone

As the Battle Group crossed the Start Line, more complications followed. First the Battle Group was cut in half by an artillery convoy of over 100 trucks, and the commander of the Reconnaissance Platoon had to threaten violence to get the remainder of the Royal's waggons through.

As we were rolling across, they came off at the right flank, from nowhere out of the dark – it was dark and raining at this point – and went straight across the front of the Battle Group. In fact, they went straight across, then they turned right so they were virtually travelling down our axis. It was unbelievable. At which point I heard what was happening on the radio, because the CO couldn't work out what was happening, so I cut off the right hand side, cut through them, stopped them, and went through them again. They carried off heading south now. [I] pitched left to try and find out who [they were], drove all the way up the front, flagged them down, went back down again to look for a command waggon and they started going off again.

Eventually I stopped the waggon right in front and I said, "Look, fucking stop, otherwise you're going to be wearing this Rardon Cannon!", or words to that effect. This guy [said], "Who the hell are you?" "1RS Battle Group. Who the Hell are you, and where are you going, why are you here? You shouldn't be here!"

I think what was happening was that because people had got the SATNAVs, instead of going by the recognized routes, the MSRs [Main Supply Routes], they were just tracking across the desert in a straight line to make the time. So they were probably doing the best thing I suppose, but the trouble is that they were unaware, as always at low level command, what part they're playing in the operation as a whole, and they were ploughing straight across the front of the Battle Group.

An armoured convoy is about two kilometres, three kilometres, long and we wouldn't have crossed it for ages, so I managed to stop them and we got the Battle Group to filter past us. [It turned out that this was] the ammunition for the operation we were crossing the line of departure for! So neither would happen without the other.

Captain Angus McLeod, Commander, Reconnaissance Platoon

Then it was discovered that because the orders had been changed and there was some confusion during the briefing, the Life Guard Squadron, the Battle Group's only tanks, had gone to the wrong "Waypoint" and they too had become entangled with another formation.

There had been confusion about Waypoints because the Brigadier had changed his orders as we crossed the border. I took the Waypoints from the orders. Not being satisfied, I then went to the Brigade Commander straight after the O Group and said, "I'm not happy with these Waypoints," and he gave me the new ones. The Squadron Leader, Jamie Hewitt, obviously hadn't got the new ones, [and] worked on the old ones. But I had time to sit back and plot where Hewitt was when he was feeding his grid references in. I then spoke to Colonel Iain and said, "Look, it looks to me as though he's spun off on the wrong track. He's gone on a wider arc and he's taken the wrong Waypoint." He was in danger of getting tied up in the 14th/20th [Hussars] Battle Group on our left. In fact he was damned nearly in front of them!

Major Kirk Gillies

B Company and the Battle Group Headquarters assembled at the correct Waypoint to await the return of the separated elements and although they were in radio contact with the Life Guards, as the tanks appeared, moving up to rejoin the Battle Group, there was some concern that this may be an Iraqi column.

I was talking to the CO on the radio. He and I went to the next Waypoint, and we waited there to reform before we moved off. A Company eventually found their way back up to us, because they had got separated, and then we waited on the tanks. I picked up some lights or vehicles moving, through my II [Image Intensifier], way out, 2 K's out to the north and [I was] just trying to talk to the tanks, although we could talk to them on the radio, and just to assure ourselves that that was them coming in and it wasn't some enemy counter-attack.

Major John Potter

It was with great relief that the Challengers were identified so, with A Company and the Recce Platoon rejoining, the force was ready to move off and the assault got under way.

Just after midnight the Life Guards reported their first contact with the enemy and fired both their main armament (120mm guns) and their machine-guns. B Company's Warriors then drew level with the tanks and their Milan section wheeled round to cover the northern flank, in case of a surprise counter-attack. The Iraqi positions were fired on by 5 and 6 Platoons with high-explosive rounds from their 30mm Rardon Cannon and with their chain guns. By 3am it appeared that the enemy might be prepared to surrender.

Major Potter, Commander of B Company, then moved along the axis of the attack, to the centre, and ordered the vehicle commanders to flash their headlights at the Iraqis.

There were really two options open, that we could get out and clear through the bunkers one by one, at night, or we could try and persuade them to come out with their hands up, and I ordered my driver and indeed 5 Platoon to flash their headlights, really to show them where we were. It was such a pitch black night, although we could look through our Image Intensifiers, they couldn't see us. You've got to be able to surrender to something. Anybody who has got the balls to flash their headlights 100 metres away from a defensive position has an air of superiority about them, and you can surrender to someone like that. It was just to give the message, "Do we go on? You either surrender or you die, and that is your choice!"

Major John Potter

At this point about five or six Iraqis decided to surrender and approached the Warriors with their hands up. This was the start of a much larger surrender and Potter moved 6 Platoon further up to take the prisoners. Some of B Company then dismounted and called in some illuminating fire from the Mortar Platoon, but the mortar line was not within range.

Major Potter called for Illum [illuminating rounds] to be fired on to BRONZE, but the mortar line was too far behind. I think they were delayed for a good twenty-five minutes while we were waiting on them catching up. They had been caught in the backlog of the other convoys and they couldnae' get through them. Because the Warriors were moving that much faster, the 432s were struggling to keep up.

We went in. The tanks hit the position first. They swept round to the side and then the company moved up. Because it was that dark you couldnae' really see what was happening, [and] we couldnae' get the support from the mortar line vehicles, Major Potter got his platoon sergeants with the 51mm Mortars, and they were putting up the smaller version of the Illumination while the Mortar line was setting up.

They eventually came up. We got them brought into action. It wasnae' the correct method of bringing them into action. All we wanted to do was just get the Illumination up in the air as fast as possible, and all we [did] was point the barrel in the direction of the enemy and adjust the round as we seen it. If it was too high we told them to lower it, if it was too low we told them to raise it. It was certainly a mixed up method of doing it, but it was the fastest way we could think. In fact, when the mortar line got there, out of the six vehicles that we started with, going through the breach, I think there was only two vehicles made it to the firing line to put the Illum down!

Sergeant Peter Fagan, Mortar Fire Controller, B Company

It was 4 and 5 Platoon's 51mm mortars which provided the light initially, so that the men on the ground could search the surrendering Iraqi soldiers.

We had them all in a line, and I was being covered by Private Julian, from Two Section. I called them forward one at a time and I got one forward, searched him and I was holding my rifle at the time and found it difficult to search him. So I told him to kneel down, hands on his head, called another one forward; he knelt down. I then put my rifle down next to Private Julian and drew my 9mm pistol, because it was a lot easier to use my pistol to search them, and cocked it, in front of their faces, not thinking. They thought I was going to execute them and the look on their faces at that moment is the lasting memory that I have, the lasting individual memory. The actual look of terror on their faces, that they thought I was going to execute them, and their life was in my hands. It was rather disturbing that anybody should think that of me. I felt quite horrified. I held the pistol slightly away and said, "No, no, OK!" and started to search them, trying not to terrify them, but we'd heard of suicide bombers and prisoners strapped up with explosive, and you've got to keep the upper hand.

We searched them then got them all in a line and started marching them back behind the Warrior. I'd got back into the Warrior and drove back towards the Company position, which was about fifteen hundred metres behind.

2nd Lieutenant Roger Walker

While Potter and his men were processing their prisoners, they discovered they were in a minefield, so movement had to be limited to the tracks made by the vehicles. An additional momentary shock was provided by one of the Iraqis who was so pleased to surrender that he tried to embrace John Potter. Mindful of a report from the Americans, warning about suicide bombers after an American soldier had been killed by a prisoner with a Claymore mine concealed in his clothing, Potter knocked him to the ground.

We were more frightened of that, of the suicide bomber. This bloody man decided to leap forward and hug me as I turned to talk to someone. I was biting and clawing and scratching and butting and everything and he went down very quickly. The top of his nose was well dented by my helmet and I was about to shoot him when I realized what it was, that he was not a suicide bomber, he was just so grateful and expressing his gratitude in the way that Arabs do, they embrace. It just wasn't the right time or the right person to embrace!

Major John Potter

Shocked!

A prisoner who spoke English revealed that they were part of a forward position, the equivalent of about two platoons in strength, and offered to show where the depth positions containing the gun emplacements were located. The gun line was about 700 metres south-east, and fire from the Warriors was directed on to it.

With B Company's guns marking the site, A Company was able to move from the south and assault the depth positions containing the guns and clear them. They too dismounted some troops to take prisoners.

What I did was I got my guys out at the side of the waggon, two teams, one either side of the waggon and we just walked forward slowly. There was a lot of firing going on from B Company and the tanks and one or two of our own motors. I kept the guys in close because it was really foul weather and I didn't want them to stray away from the protection of the waggon. "Just walk along with the motor. If we get a contact we'll shake out and deal with it."

I think the whole Battle Group at that time were up forward. [They] switched the [head] lights on – some tactic, I would never use it myself! – but they switched the lights on so that we could see them coming, and if they were going to surrender they knew where to come.

As we got a bit closer we shouted "Halt!" in Arabic; they all stopped. We told them to get down, called them forward one at a time into the shade where they couldn't see us, frisked them, took them down the side and separated the officers from the soldiers. They were really scared; you could tell it was pure fear in the faces; they thought we would have wasted them there and then. That's probably the type of thing they would have done if they'd captured us. They'd taken some beating for about an hour beforehand and just decided to give in. It was six officers and just two normal soldiers, *Jundi* I think they call them. We tried to get a lot of information out of them. They were really scared, I couldn't believe the state they were in either, no boots, they were in their bare feet. It was absolutely freezing. We had our full combats on; we had the NBC suits on, fragmentation jackets on plus our webbing on top of that. We thought it was pretty cold with the rain and everything else, and these people were walking with a shirt that's not tied up properly, their trousers are hanging on them and there's nothing on their feet. This is the officers and the soldiers as well!

We wanted to know where the gun positions were so that the Forward Observation Officer could inspect their ammunition to see if it was of a chemical nature. I was getting information off them, passing it to the vehicle commander who was sending it over the net to Major Soutar. In turn he was letting the IO [Intelligence Officer] know, and the IO came up.

Corporal Billy Paul

I went forward to A Company. I think it was one of their right forward sections, and we got about eight or nine prisoners. We knew where the gun positions were. They'd just walked from one of their gun positions through the anti-personnel mines. They were scared. Obviously there was [such] a pounding they were glad to surrender. They were very surprised when a white man came up and spoke Arabic to them. [Of] course, all the Jocks had been shouting at them, giving it lots of "Hands up, do this, do that" "Simon says", that sort of [thing]. But when I came up and spoke Arabic it was a real shock to them. They thought we were Israeli for a while and someone speaking Arabic to them was an added disconcerting factor. They told us about this minefield that was around. They were willing to take us back through to where their guns were for a Warrior to take them out. And their officers, very happy to talk; talk their heads off. This guy took us round to his gun site. No coercion, [no] marching him back at bayonet point, "No, no, I will take you!" They were in a pretty bad state, pretty badly shaken up and they were all dirty. They hadn't been looking after themselves at all. We weren't the cleanest specimens at that stage, but they were really run down.

Captain Dermot Fulton

Altogether about a hundred prisoners were taken and while the Rifle Companies remounted to move off for the next objective some men were left behind to make absolutely certain that the equipment on the site was completely destroyed.

Once it got daylight, the companies were going on to their next objective. I then got a Bergen full of grenades and an Iraqi prisoner who spoke English. He said there was three people missing, so we went round bunker to bunker with this Iraqi calling them out to see if they were in there and as I went round I just blew up any vehicles that were there. Something like five vehicles I destroyed, just put grenades in the petrol tanks.

The Iraqi had actually been educated in England and he'd been dragged out of his village to go and fight, didnae' want to fight – although they all say that – but he was very helpful. He went to the bunkers, because of the chance of booby traps; he did the business for us; he went round every bunker getting the rifles out, checking there was nobody in there, and on that side, the eastern side of the position there wasnae' anybody in there. I says, "Well where are these three people?" Couldn't find them. I said, "They must be dead."

So we left it at that, I put him back with the rest of the prisoners and then I went over on the western side because there was some Flak[8] guns there which looked undamaged, the quad guns, the ZSU 4s. So I went over there with a Warrior and I told the Warrior commander to go and put AP [Armour Piercing ammunition] through every one of the guns.

We moved further north-west on the position and I could see three helmets and three pairs of boots just outside of a bunker. Somebody'd been awfully neat and tidy before they went. So we went up to the bunker and I jumped into the trench and as I jumped in I pulled the night blanket they had over them to keep out the light, and as I went forward this black face [appeared] right in front of me, and it was an Iraqi sitting there. I don't know who was the more surprised, him or me! I took a pace back, took a grenade out to throw it in and then I heard, "No, don't shoot, don't shoot, don't shoot!" In fact there was three of them in there in the bunker, and it took about twenty minutes to convince them that we werenae' going to kill them, to get them out of the trench. Eventually we got them out of the trench and took them back.

These were the three we were looking for; they'd deserted to the other position. The only reason they had boots was they took them off corpses the night before, and one guy the only reason he had a uniform was he had took it off a corpse. Before he was in civvies. They'd just whipped him off his village.

He was told that we were going to take no prisoners, plus he thought we were Israelis and then we convinced him that we werenae'. We tried to convince him that we were Scottish, but that was too much for them, so we just said "We're English", to keep it simple. When I told him we werenae' going to kill him, and the war was over for him, to use the cliche, he then started to kiss my feet and call me a God. I said, "I'm not a God, I'm a Sergeant Major, but it's the nearest thing you're going to see to a God!"

WO2 Dave Dickson

As the men remounted their Warriors a message was received from the Life Guards that an armoured column was to the north. The Challengers' Thermal Imaging equipment could pick up the heat signature of a substantial number of armoured vehicles, but it was impossible to get a profile and make a positive identification. The Commanding Officer asked the Operations Officer to contact Brigade Headquarters, and he was assured that no friendly forces were in the area so it seemed as though this could be Iraqi reinforcements and a possible counter-attack. In accordance with its standard procedure the Battle Group lined up and selected targets. The total fire power was staggering, 14 Challenger Tanks, 18 Warrior AFVs, 3 Milan firing posts and a whole regiment of Artillery – 24 guns, with A Company and two more Milan sections on the way up. They were capable of destroying the entire column in seconds. However, something did not seem right. Again the Operations Officer called Brigade, and again he was assured that there should be no friendly forces in the area.

We left BRONZE and, just swinging up to BRASS, we hit another infantry position which we weren't expecting; it had about fifty armoured vehicles behind it. We knew exactly where those fifty vehicles were because we lased[9] them; there were supposed to be no enemy there and we confirmed about three or four times that the area was clear. There were no friendly forces there; therefore it must be the enemy. It didn't seem right and we didn't engage those armoured vehicles and let them escape because we just weren't happy about it.

Lt.Colonel Iain Johnstone

The Iraqi position, discovered at the time that the armoured column had been spotted, which was on the southern tip of objective COPPER, contained a Mortar Locating Platoon. Under ferocious artillery bombardment they had tried to dig shell scrapes with their bare hands and were in a very sorry state when they finally surrendered at about 4.30 in the morning. There were four dead and three wounded men on the position. The Battle Group was under pressure from Brigade to press on to their main task, objective BRASS, and there was still some concern that the armoured column may turn out to be Iraqis and may still launch a counter-attack. As it happened, the news eventually came through that the armoured column had been identified. It was a British Mobile Dressing Station which, like the wayward artillery column encountered earlier, was presumably travelling "as the crow flies" using SATNAV, and had strayed into a potentially dangerous situation.

Once we'd got around the problem of this bloody Dressing Station we still had the infantry position. As dawn broke they packed it in and we found out later that they were a Mortar Locating Platoon or troop we'd caught in the open and we'd killed about four of them and wounded about five and the rest were in no state to go on and they wrapped it in. But it also provided us with the first real sight of what our weapons were capable of and it's an image that will certainly stick with me for the rest of my life.

Major John Potter

We took out the infantry position which surrendered at first light and there were a lot of injured there. That was my dilemma, what to do with the injured [Iraqis]. I still had to press on and so we took them with us, stuck them in the ambulances and carried on, because I didn't want to leave any ambulances behind. At that stage we were only two or three kilometres to the north of a couple of Iraqi Divisions that had not been addressed.

Lt.Colonel Iain Johnstone

Under pressure to press on, but with Iraqi casualties to deal with, Iain Johnstone left Kirk Gillies and part of the Regimental Aid Post, including the Padre, to tidy up at BRONZE.

I got left behind because the CO was keen to push further on to meet the timings for BRASS. He was under great pressure from Brigade, but at that stage I had to be a little bit terse with him on the radio, and we both laughed about it afterwards, but I had to remind him that we had an obligation under the Geneva Convention to patch these poor bastards up and they were in some shape. So I stayed behind with half the RAP to make sure they were patched up and then I pushed on.

Major Kirk Gillies

Treating and stabilizing the Iraqi casualties so that they could be moved was done by B Company's Medics, Lance-Corporal Meechan and Private Blake. The injuries and wounds suffered by the Iraqi wounded and dead were recorded as follows:

Casualty 1 – GSW [Gunshot wound] to right leg, multiple wounds to lower right leg, hit about 8 times with both entry and exit wounds. Both tibia and fibula were smashed. Two entry and exit wounds on right thigh with broken femur. One wound centre of abdominal region. No exit wound. Eleven FFD [First Field Dressings] were applied with one syrette of morphine and an IV drip was set up. The casualty survived.

Casualty 2 – Shrapnel wound to right shoulder. Treated with FFD.

Casualty 3 – Two GSW to back, right side of chest with entry and exit wounds. Treated with 4 × FFD and an IV drip set up.

The dead were consistent with the effect of HE [High Explosive]. These were:

a. Hit in face by 30mm (?). No facial features left. Death instantaneous.

b. Hit in face and chest by 30mm HE. No facial features left. 4″ hole in left side of chest. Death instantaneous.

c. Hit in chest by 120mm HESH (?). No chest left. Death instantaneous.

d. Blast injuries consistent with 120mm HESH. No external injuries visible. Death instantaneous.

B Company Diary

Burial of the Iraqi dead became the responsibility of the Padre.

I got out of the back of the vehicle and I was in a bit of a daze because it was the first time I'd been out of the vehicle for about twelve hours or something, and looked around, and it was an amazing scene, and there was so much to take in and I wandered about for a few minutes and someone said, "There are some dead bodies". And it took two to three minutes before it clicked that actually my job was now to bury these dead because we hadn't got long and we shouldn't just leave them there. So I got some of the lads to help me and we gathered all the dead bodies together and a tractor came up and dug the trench. One of the Iraqi officers, [who] spoke a little bit of English, asked us if they could do the service. So we helped him to line up the bodies facing Mecca and he did the service and threw in the first couple of handfuls of earth and we covered them over. He was very grateful for that, he gave me a big hug. He was very pleased, for his mates, that he had been able to give them a decent burial.

Major Stephen Blakey

While Kirk Gillies was making his way from BRONZE towards BRASS, he was surprised to find himself taking prisoners.

I was going along with the Headquarters and we passed through a position on the main track with lots of old tank scrapes, where they'd scraped the sand away so that tanks could hide in them. I had my head out of the turret, I looked over my left shoulder and saw an arm in one of these scrapes. I put my head back in and said, "Poor bastard" to Corporal Tate, the gunner. My mind then started playing on, "No, that's not quite right", so I said, "Stop". We stopped the vehicle and I got on the radio to Sergeant-Major Gallagher, the Mortar Second-in-Command, behind me, and I said, "Look, check that scrape beside your motor."

Sergeant-Major Gallagher had been involved in a scrape the night before, some rounds had hit his vehicle from somewhere. So he got out of his vehicle and was looking round it. I said, "What the hell are you doing, looking round your vehicle?" He said, "I'm checking my motor for a scrape!"

Anyway, at that stage, Sergeant-Major Butler, Two I/C of the Anti-Tank Platoon, had noticed that out of this tank-scrape was crawling some Iraqis, so he was fumbling for his weapon. He couldn't get his gun out quick enough! These nine Iraqi officers had been hiding, clearly having deserted their men. I think they may have been from BRONZE, the one that we had just shot up. These guys were obviously trying to abscond; they came out and surrendered to us. They were saying, "Thank you for your invitation, we got your invitation." I thought, "I don't remember any bloody invitation!" but they were waving these things the B52s had dropped, these little leaflets. One of them spoke English and they were offering us briefcases full of Dinar, so one of them was obviously a paymaster of some kind. Whether they were Brigade Staff or not I don't know, but one of them was a Lieutenant Colonel. They were in bits, they were cold and they'd obviously buggered off and left their men behind. So we assured them we weren't Israelis, we weren't going to shoot them, gave them some chocolate and then the RQMS came along and put them "in the bag".

Major Kirk Gillies

Back in their waggons, the men in the rifle companies had little time to consider what they had achieved. They had survived their first contact with the enemy without the expected high casualties, indeed no one in the entire Battle Group had even been wounded. Many of them had debussed and taken prisoners, but it was still too soon to know whether this would be typical or whether they would still encounter Saddam Hussein's "Mother of All Battles".

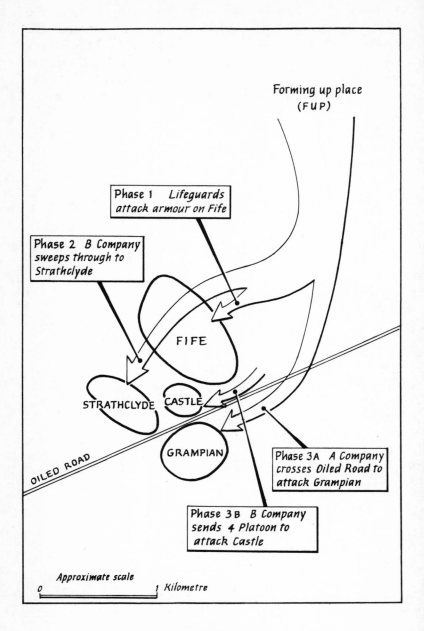

Forming up place (FUP)

Phase 1 Lifeguards attack armour on Fife

Phase 2 B Company sweeps through to Strathclyde

FIFE

STRATHCLYDE CASTLE

GRAMPIAN

OILED ROAD

Phase 3A A Company crosses Oiled Road to attack Grampian

Phase 3B B Company sends 4 Platoon to attack Castle

Approximate scale
0 ————————— 1 Kilometre

Chapter 4

THE PLAN

We had a plan for that. I say that because it's the only plan we ever had during the war. We'd thought about it, we'd analysed it, we'd made our own maps from air photographs, and everybody right down to the most junior soldier had been briefed on it; and it worked like clockwork.

Lt.Colonel Iain Johnstone

OBJECTIVE BRASS

Now came the Royal Scots' main objective, the one they had been briefed for originally. Code-named BRASS, it was a large and complex defensive position thought to contain some three or four tanks and ten to fifteen armoured personnel carriers, all of them dug in, as well as anti-aircraft artillery used in a direct-fire role as anti-tank weapons and, inevitably, trenches manned by infantry. It was therefore divided up among the Battle Group and, not surprisingly from a Scottish unit, the individual objectives were assigned the code-names FIFE, STRATHCLYDE, CASTLE and GRAMPIAN.

We'd given the objectives names, which we used. We were going to give them the Company Commanders' Christian names, but we thought it would not go down in history very well to have objective NORMAN and objective JOHN! And if we'd actually decided for A Company to attack B Company's position, it would have been very confusing.

Lt.Colonel Iain Johnstone

The front of this position faced almost due west, roughly towards the Iraq/Saudi border. It was to be assaulted from the rear, ensuring the essential element of surprise and dealing with the greatest threat – the Iraqi tanks – first.

We went up north and swung round on 180 degrees which is something only Satellite Navigation could allow us to do. We'd just gone round the position and were about to attack at the back.

Lt.Colonel Iain Johnstone

FIFE was the area thought to contain tanks so that would be dealt with by James Hewitt's Life Guards Squadron. B Company of the Royal Scots would then attack STRATH-CLYDE, and CASTLE and cross an oiled road to give fire support to A Company in its attack on GRAMPIAN.

While the Battle Group was on its way from Objective BRONZE to the Startline for this next assault, a barrage from the Multiple Launch Rocket System of the Royal Artillery was hitting the Iraqi positions at BRASS. These positions had also been subjected to a US Airforce A10 airstrike.

The Royal Scots Battle Group crossed the Startline at 8.11am and advanced in formation with the Life Guards leading the way. The dust thrown up by the artillery bombardment was whipped about by high winds reducing visibility to less than 100 metres, even on the Challengers' Thermal Imaging equipment. This meant that the Battle Group's Warriors could easily be within range of the Iraqi tanks' main guns before visual contact was made.

The artillery barrage had come down, and you could see virtually nothing whatsoever, and Andy [Shearer – the MFC who was working forward] says he couldnae' record any targets. So we were sitting, the tanks were sitting, the mortar line was sitting. The mortars werenae' firing at that stage so we knew the tanks were sweeping off, coming in round from one of the flanks, and the Companies were the next to go in.

Well I was sitting behind one of the platoons who was to take the first location. They were waiting on the orders to move forward. We knew there was nobody in front of us, our own troops, 'cause we knew the tanks had pulled away, so we just gave the mortar line a grid to fire on. They were just doing harassing fire, just getting the rounds down. As we started moving forward I remember passing by the mortar line, and you could see the guys actually firing the rounds, and they were throwing the rounds down the barrel as if they was going out of fashion. It was a good sight. When A Company moved in, they actually moved in with the rounds still coming in on the ground.

Sergeant Peter Fagan

The Life Guards reported no sign of any tanks on Objective FIFE, so B Company moved up on to its firing line in its standard configuration with 5 Platoon on the left, 6 Platoon on the right, John Potter's Command vehicle in the centre, and 4 Platoon in reserve.

STRATHCLYDE was the Warriors' target, but before they could engage, an urgent message came through from the Challengers. An Iraqi tank had been spotted.

As we got into the firing line the tanks reported a contact with a T55 starting to reverse out of emplacements, and I was therefore stuck between our tanks and the Iraqi tanks, and with people firing on TI [Thermal Imaging] it certainly wasn't a good place to be. I pulled the Company back about 400 metres until the tanks reported that they'd knocked it out. I think they'd taken five T55s by then.

Major John Potter

The vehicles were aligned, three up, one back. . . . I had Callsign Three-one on my left, Callsign Three-two on my right and Callsign Three-three behind me. The tanks that came up said, "We've seen [Iraqi] tanks moving on the position," so John Potter immediately told us to "get the fuck out of there!" We went into reverse and we moved back behind the tanks. The tanks then continued the motion, then said, "OK, you're clear, move back in," and we continued to blast them and brass them up.

2nd Lieutenant Roger Walker

Time 0905. Am waiting in FUP. Tanks already destroyed X 4 T-55 and elements of dug-in Infantry. B Coy going in now. Then A, then me & Milan to secure L [left] flank.

Lieutenant Guy Richardson

As 6 Platoon's Warriors moved round to take their next objective, the precise configuration and location of their target was not entirely clear.

We'd been brassing them up and we'd been seeing trenches. I thought OK fine, we've seen all the trenches, blasted all the trenches we've seen, blasted all the hard targets that we'd seen. By this time I was sort of feeling relaxed. I then got the word, "This is Zero Bravo [the Company Commander], continue on your objective as planned."

Now I couldn't see my objective. I could see the enemy position in the big scale, but there was no way that I could identify what was my position, the position I was meant to be taking. I was meant to be taking out a platoon position or a company headquarters position with what was thought to be a platoon guard, and the other two platoons, 4 and 5, were to take out the battle group headquarters with probably about a company guard.

Now I didn't know whether I was directly in front of the battle group headquarters, in which case if I had gone in with my four waggons against a company, we couldn't have stood much of a chance. I could have gone in between them and been sandwiched from either side. I didn't know where I was, so I came back and said, "Cannot identify my objective." "Well," he said, "It's to your front!" I said, "Roger, all I can see is an earth mound spreading from my left arc, all the way across as far as you can see to the right where it builds up and turns a right angle." He said "Roger", paused and then he came back, "Right we'll by-pass this one, A Company can take their objective and we'll come back and clear it when the mist's gone."

2nd Lieutenant Roger Walker

The Plan

As A Company received the command to move in, the navigation satellite went down. They were to cross an oiled road and swing round on to the position, attacking in a well-planned formation, following closely behind mortar and artillery fire.

"Is this the tarred [oiled] road?" "I don't know. What do you think?" We swung right at that stage and we were initially going to have two platoons up and what we did find was that because they had ten guys in the back, [and] all their ammunition, they had an extra pull on the engine. We found ourselves out in front. So there was the Company Commander's vehicle literally leading from the front. We must have been two hundred metres ahead of everybody else. Norman said, "Not enough, not enough, get Three [platoon] up, get Three up!" and the platoon at the back swung round and we fanned out in a huge line, a long line of about twenty vehicles, and we sort of drew back, and realized at this stage, this is it. It was like a late twentieth century cavalry charge!

We went through and I saw red flashes in the sky above us. It was mortar fire being called down, mortar or artillery fire being called down on the enemy position, which gave us a clue to the location, and it was going so fast there wasn't time to call it off. So it was a case of quick combat appreciation; what do you do? Bloody well drive through it! Keep going through it!

[We] finally swung them all through. Three platoons on the left engaged some MTLBs on the move and I remember going in and Norman saying, "I've got two guns [in my sights]. I've got two guns. Can you hit them?" They were anti-aircraft pieces which had been moved down to fire in a ground role, I had visions of 88s, like the Afrika Korps[1], so I destroyed them and then cracked on, by which stage this huge line just swept through the Iraqi position. It must have been horrifying for them to see that coming towards them.

Lieutenant Chris Brannigan

As A Company bore down on the Iraqi positions one of the Sections of 1 Platoon even opened the vehicle mortar hatches, despite the danger from bursting artillery shells, and fired its machine guns on the way in.

The great thing for me was – we'd been discussing with Corporal Cohen's section, on my left-hand side, the possibility of opening the mortar hatches and using the GPMGs, because there were two GPMG gunners in the back of his waggon, as an extra bit of firepower. Instead of having just one 7.62[2] why can't we have three? I said "Well, that's a great idea, entirely up to your discretion if you want to, it's a brave man that gets out, sticks out the top!" During the attack, [I recall] looking left and seeing exactly that, two Jocks up the top, absolutely tremendous, totally committed to it. So there was this great weight of firepower going down there. It was just after the artillery barrage as well, with all the explosions around them, they'd just opened the mortar hatches and come out so they must have been completely dedicated to what they were doing. It was a great feeling for a commander to see that.
Lieutenant Kenny Douglas, Commander, 1 Platoon, A Company

While the rest of A Company pressed on to engage the depth positions, a section from 2 Platoon, in Callsign Two-three, the vehicle to the extreme right of the Company's advance, prepared to debus to force a surrender from the smashed Iraqi positions.

My motor was the extreme right one so we could hear all the shit from B Company and the Life Guards as well, and I can remember at this stage just looking round the guys. Well, this is the big one. We knew fine that we were going to get out, that we were going to stop and get out and do some real soldiering, as they call it. I *thought* that we were going to take casualties, and I knew fine that we were going to encounter some small arms fire or maybe RPG[3]. So we were trundling along, well absolutely horsing along and I'm trying to speak to the commander, saying, "Try and get us into a bit of cover, when we get to debus." This is me trying to get a bit of cover first and then try and look after the section, and at least get ourselves organized first and then mount a section attack. But as I was saying that, in the turret he says, "There's nothing out there, there's nothing out there to cover you at all!" We'd seen the air photographs and all that, but you don't know what the hell you're going to see when you get out there. When I get out of the back of the waggon, if there's somebody shooting at me, that's the only intelligence I'm going to take heed of.

I asked for a count-down from the commander, and I told some of the guys to fix bayonets, some not, and he gave us a count-down, "Hundred metres to go, fifty metres to go, they're coming at us, they're coming at us!" But we didn't know whether they were firing at us or not. The waggon stopped; we got out of the back. I don't know whether the vehicle was firing or not. My section dismounted. Andy McLean, he's my gunner, he was first out with the GPMG, so he lets rip at whatever's out there. "If there's nothing happening out there that's fine but," I just says, "Get out there!" He got out of the box at two hundred and he just let rip, didn't bother – "Don't look for targets, just get out there and spray. That'll keep their heads [down] and give us time!"

So we shook out and there they were, quite a lot of people coming towards us, quite a lot of Iraqis, but they'd downed tools, sacked it for the day – "I don't want any more of this!" Anything white at all they were grabbing hold of. Trying to kiss the guys. I wouldn't let them come any closer. I fired a few volley shots in the air because they were starting to piss me off, the way they were jumping about, and I'm thinking "Booby traps, booby traps!" This is what's going through my head, they were trying to get in amongst the guys. A couple of shots in the air, "Get down where you are!" [and] we called them forward one at a time.

Corporal Billy Paul

While B Company's 4 Platoon cleared through Objective CASTLE, 6 Platoon accompanied by Captain Alex Alderson, the Company Second-in-Command, provided supporting fire for A Company's assault. John Potter took 5 Platoon back to the position that had been by-passed on the way in, to force a surrender of the Iraqis that were left there.

We were then told to go back and clear, physically, the objective that we had just come through. We saw four people in a trench who were taking no physical action against us, yet at the same time were not making any motion to surrender. These were engaged by Callsign Two-one with HE and Co-ax and they disappeared down into the trench system. I then moved forward with Two-one still mounted towards the trench that we'd seen the activity from. They then came up and waved a white flag attached to an AK47. From previous actions we then expected no further aggression from the enemy. Which indeed is what we got. These guys were in the forward trench of a series of Company Headquarters-type trench systems. I dismounted Two-one to go take them prisoner. In the act of so doing, we then saw an MTLB to the rear of them, ten, twenty metres up towards what was obviously the command trench. I'd elected not to dismount at this point as I only wanted Two-one to take prisoners.

On dismounting and moving forward to take the prisoners they saw the MTLB and the command trench and quite correctly off their own initiative started moving forward to neutralize that position. As I had not dismounted my other two sections, they were not in a position to help them at this point.

I did not want that to happen, and attempted to call back that section so that the mounted Warriors could, with their own direct-fire weapons, give the trench a fairly good blasting before they moved forward to ensure the trench was clear. Communication was the problem really. I was sitting there with the headset on; they had got out into a position which we had been informed previously could have held three or four hundred people and were moving forward to eliminate any possible aggression. At the same time I wanted them to pull back and take prisoners. It all turned, as I suppose these things do, into a bit of a dog's bollocks.

Lieutenant Alastair Stobie

Although it was thought that all the Iraqi vehicles had been destroyed, one which was particularly well dug-in had apparently survived the withering fire poured down by the Warriors.

As we got in, [Callsign] Two-one spotted a position right in front of the vehicle and there was fire coming from that position, bouncing off the driver's hatch. They were tasked to debus. As we got into the process of debussing, then the trench raised a white flag and we debussed to take the prisoners under the white flag. Two of the prisoners came out and the other three were sort of reluctant, but we got them out.

Because there was prisoners involved I debussed to take the prisoners with Two-one. It was then we spotted the MTLB, with the machine-gun and that's why they just swung and engaged that.

The Platoon Commander leads the attack on the ground. It's just that I was in the wrong place at the right time. Normally he would have debussed himself, taken the prisoners, then I would have debussed once the prisoners were rounded up. That's why I was on the ground in the attack and not the Platoon Commander. He was in the turret at that stage.

Sergeant Tom Gorrian

It was Private Gow, who had been detailed by the Company Commander to take some prisoners to the rear, who suddenly noticed the turret of the very well-concealed MTLB starting to traverse towards the section. He screamed for the rest of the Jocks to "Get fucking back here!" and fired a CLAW rifle grenade at the vehicle, which blew up as he threw in a white phosphorous hand grenade to finish it off.

[We] debussed and that's where the other bunkers were. I'd just seen a turret, the MTLB, and it was traversing and my section was spread away out, a couple of my guys were taking prisoners back. I was screaming, "Get fucking back here!" That was when the O/C was right behind us. I'd seen the guys debussing up there and I just fired a CLAW at this MTLB and moved forward. It exploded before I grenaded it. I sprayed it and that was it.

Private Tom Gow

As Gow crawled closer he could see two bunkers, still manned by Iraqi troops, so, calling for covering fire, he moved towards them. At this point Private Steel, the GPMG gunner of the section, had a stoppage. As he struggled to clear it, Gow pressed on and threw a grenade at the trench containing the bunkers. At the crucial moment, however, the strap on the yoke of his web equipment caught across his upper arm causing the grenade to fall short. He threw another grenade, which burst on the bunkers; then he sprayed them with automatic fire from his SA80.

Later some of the men went in to look at the bunkers. In the entrance to one lay a severed hand. One of the NCOs covered it with a discarded Iraqi helmet.

I went back with 5 Platoon to clear the rest of Objective STRATHCLYDE, specifically the Company Headquarters area, where one of the APCs [Armoured Personnel Carriers] had been dug in so deeply, being used as a command post, that we couldn't engage it with cannon. We dismounted and commenced clearing through the bunkers to get towards the vehicle and that was the point where Private Gow won his Military Medal. There was a great deal of confusion. It was slowing down and he took the initiative and went forward on his own. The area was covered in bomblets; there was an anti-personnel mine threat; he crawled to about 20 metres from the vehicle and hit it with the Close Assault Weapon – CLAW – rifle grenade. It started to burn and he followed it up with a white-phosphorous grenade. He then went forward and cleared another two bunkers around it, until I called him off, because at that point a lot of ammunition was exploding around us from the [Iraqi] vehicle, and I didn't want him to waste time on that. In fact, if I hadn't stopped him at that point, God knows where he'd have ended up.

Major John Potter

All of a sudden we were in a situation where somebody wanted a fight, and we were there to give them it. It paid off in the end.

Sergeant Tom Gorrian

At last the position was secure and the prisoners were handed over to RSM Frazer's PoW handling section for transport back to one of the camps that had been set up. The shock of capture is a well-known phenomenon which often gives a psychological advantage to interrogators seeking information from Prisoners of War. However, the pitiful state of some of the prisoners provoked feelings of compassion among even the hardest Jocks who were soon offering cigarettes, food and water to the Iraqis, after the necessary searches had been completed. While this attitude was laudable in humanitarian terms, it was not in the best traditions of professional soldiering and could have been a potentially dangerous reaction while there were other objectives to be taken, and other targets to be hit, so the men were quickly reminded that these were enemy soldiers and the war had not yet been won.

Although the Royal Scots had not actually taken on any Republican Guard formations, there were certainly some individual members among the prisoners that they captured, presumably attached to the Iraqi units manning BRASS in an effort to stiffen them.

The five prisoners we took on BRASS when we did the attack, they were [Republican] Guard Force. They were pleading with [the men from Callsign] Two-one not to shoot them. Two-one didn't make any aggressive move to indicate they were going to shoot, [but] the guys were praying to God, "Don't shoot, don't shoot!" You can understand the way they felt.

They were standing about in a line; you've got to split them straightaway. The guys would just grab them, pull them over, tell them to get down, that sort of thing and start searching them. We found that doing that and asking questions at the same time, because the prisoner was in disarray he didn't know what your intentions were and what you were going to do to him. He spilt quite a lot, and once he started [talking], you take him aside, speak to him nicely. You slide your weapon round your back so your weapon was out of sight and you just speak to him, and we found he gave quite a lot. It worked quite a few times. But the officers weren't hard to pick out; they stood out like sore thumbs. They had boots; they were always better dressed than the privates.

Sergeant Tom Gorrian

During a pre-Gulf lecture about Prisoners of War some of the officers had been advised on how they could identify Iraqi officers who had removed their rank insignia. They had been told that anyone wearing a watch was likely to be an officer. But the prevailing apocryphal story is that a certain test was to get them to drop their trousers. Anyone who was wearing underwear was definitely an officer!

Not all of the Rifle Platoons' Warriors went into the assault on BRASS. Callsign Two-zero, the command vehicle of 2 Platoon, A Company, shed a track on the move up. It was carrying, along with the Platoon Commander [Lieutenant Henry Angus], the Platoon Sergeant, a signaller, deputy vehicle commander, gunner and a driver. Because the driver of a Warrior sits to the left of the vehicle he has a limited field of vision and is particularly vulnerable to problems on his right, effectively his blind side, especially when the vehicle is "closed down". As Callsign Two-zero was approaching the Forming Up Point for BRASS, it came to a ditch and there was a steep bank of sand which grew steeper to the right of the vehicle's path. The driver tried to negotiate these obstacles under the directions of Lt. Angus, but the vehicle banked too steeply and a track came unlinked. This led to an extraordinary experience for the junior members of the vehicle crew.

Because it would take the REME fitters more than fifteen minutes to fix the track, Major Soutar decided that Lt. Angus and the Platoon Sergeant [Crosbie] would travel on with the Battle Group and that the rest of the crew would return to the vehicle.

By this time it was starting to get first light, so they dropped us off and just drove away and left the four of us, myself [David

Gibb], John Charge, Nick Roddam and Stan Thornton. Because it was [in] an ex-battlefield, we checked the vehicle and checked about the area and there was nothing there. John, the driver, decided let's get on with the track so Stan went in his turret for top cover. We took our webbing and weapons off and started getting in at the track.

Nick went away to do something and as he came back he goes, "There's some Iraqis out there!" And me and John casually strolled round and all we seen was this mass of bodies! "Oh shit!"

Because he was looking the other way, Stan [in the turret] twirled round onto them, Nick went out to the right, I was in the middle near the vehicle and John went to the other side. I started giving a SITREP to Captain Bruce. I didn't go straight through to the Company Commander because I knew that they were going in for an attack.

They were about five or six hundred metres away still. As they got closer we realized there were two white flags and we ended up with twelve [prisoners]. We had two officers and the rest were other ranks.

We split them all up and this is where all the training came in. It all just clicked and we flowed through it. At one point we were doing this Private and he had a lot of money. He'd opened up his wallet, he put the money down at his feet and a gust of wind came up and blew it all over me and right past me! Anyone's first reaction if their money goes is to try and get up, so this was [nearly] this guy's biggest mistake, he tried to get up. I was about to pull the trigger and Nick was grabbing him trying to calm him down. He calmed down and he realized that he'd lost his money. He'd lost everything anyway, so he may as well just leave it.

Private David Gibb

While they were considering how best to cover the prisoners and get their vehicle track back on, other allied vehicles passed periodically, so each time Private Gibb went out and flagged them down in an effort to get some support, or just to pass the prisoners on so that they could get their own waggon fixed and take part in the assault on BRASS. But everyone that stopped had their own tasks and priorities and could spare neither time nor manpower. A Mortar Platoon vehicle commander, whose 432 was under tow by the Battalion's LAD, promised to tell someone where they were. Later a passing US Artillery formation gave them a SATNAV grid reference to relay to Captain Bruce.

He gave us a ten figure grid reference of where we were, so "cheers!", at least that's better than nothing. I then encoded it and sent it up to Captain Bruce, I told him where we were, he [said], "We know where you are". The REME had told him the grid reference, 'cause they had the SATNAV. "Well, if you know where we are, why are we no out of here?"

We started trying to talk to [the prisoners] to get information out of them. There were some very bad stories. One of them showed us his house key. He says, "I had this key and I was going into my house." [One of us said], "Well, why have you [still] got it?" He was a schoolteacher. He says, "They came and got me and said if I don't come with them they'll kill [my] wife and kids!" There was another one that came straight from the Iran front. He was supposed to be finished with the Army, [but they] brought him straight down there. There was quite a few spoke English. They wanted to go to Saudi. They didn't want to go back to Iraq.

Private David Gibb

Private Gibb's last encounter with a passing Allied vehicle, this time an American patrol, was even more frustrating, and potentially quite dangerous, when he was mistaken for an Iraqi.

I went out to them, running out with my weapon as ʌsual. It was one of the [engineer] vehicles and a Landrover and they just slammed on the brakes. All I heard was cocking weapons and they were all pointing at me! I absolutely stopped, froze still and one of the guys shouted over, "Are you British?" I said, "Yes, I'm Scottish!" They [motioned] to tell me to get down, so I got down on the ground. I moved away from my weapon and they started coming out, and they were covering me.

So I was on the ground, I was fuming! They eventually got up to me, one of them had picked up my rifle and the other started playing around with my chest webbing at the back. He says to his mate, "How do you undo this?" I said, "Just undo the fucking clip!" I was really angry, because of the way I was getting treated. They thought I was an Iraqi. He goes, "Are you British?" I goes, "Aye, I'm British!" He goes, "Oh sorry mate", and helped me up.

I just grabbed my rifle with my right hand and goes "You're arseholes ain't you!"

They were all apologetic and at this time, as they were helping me up, the Warrior had just been fixed and it was charging out towards them. Nick and John thought I'd got shot. I was about four or five hundred metres away, the wind was blowing from where they were towards me so they wouldn't have heard much. So they were charging up and they were going to open up on them. Once they saw me getting up they started to slow down.

After rounding up some more prisoners, including three officers, the Americans went on their way, leaving Gibb and his comrades to guard them.

We now had seventeen prisoners; four of us! Eventually about half past three we [saw] a vehicle coming towards us. It was our Two-four Alpha, which was our LAD [Light Aid Detachment]. This Staff Sergeant got off and his first priority was what's happened to the vehicle. He had a look at it and congratulated the driver 'cause he'd done a good job, mostly by himself.

He tried to take command of the prisoners and was walking like John Wayne down the prisoners, looking at them at each side, like a right cowboy!

He says, "Right, we'll take you back to the Company." His vehicle went first, a couple of his men were on the back, weapons pointing at the prisoners. Our vehicle was at the rear and we noticed more Iraqis and we ended up with about sixty of them.

We tabbed into the Company, this was about ten or fifteen kilometres. Once we got there, everyone was getting out of their vehicles and taking photos of us. It was just like in a movie. So we got in, went straight towards the Company Commander's vehicle and I reported to him. He says to me, "Which ones speak

English?" I was walking round just pointing them all out, and they thought they were going to get shot or something, and they were getting moved forward and split up. So the English-speaking ones were out at the front and the OC ended up taking it from there and briefing them, and we got back to our platoon.

So that was an exciting day for us!

Private David Gibb

Everyone in the company was very impressed with the way the crew of Two-zero, and particularly Private Gibb, had tackled this situation.

During our move up young Private Gibb kept sending us SITREPS to let us know what was happening, and it became clear that, as they were preparing the vehicle for recovery and repair, they were taking prisoners. They kept quiet during our entire assault which was commendable restraint and common sense, because we had contacts on the go.

At the end of it they'd taken a lot of prisoners, seventy to eighty. So by the time the REME recovery vehicle got there, the vehicle was completely made ready by the driver for repair. Repair was completed very quickly, and between the REME and Private Gibb, they marched back Gibb's prisoners to the Battalion Prisoner of War cage.

Private Gibb was subsequently Mentioned in Despatches for his level-headed common sense, gutsy behaviour and example of command and control way above and beyond what is expected of a private soldier. I think had the Iraqis really wanted to fight there, they could have done, had Private Gibb not been so absolutely awe-inspiring. He ordered these boys around, he took the initiative straight from them, he had them down on their faces before they knew what was happening and that's where they stayed, until help came, and they were marched in front of the vehicles. The vehicles drove behind with their machine-guns trained on the prisoners.

Captain Robert Bruce

33. No.5 Platoon B Company attacks a dug-in MTLB on Obective BRASS. Private Gow, who spotted the dug-in Iraq MTLB. (*Mike Moore*)

34. Sergeant Gorrian (centre) calls for covering fire as Private Gow goes forward. (*Mike Moore*)

35. The MTLB burns as Gow throws another grenade in. (*Mike Moore*)

36. The grenade bursts into a sheet of flame. (*Mike Moore*)

37. Major John Potter prepares to search the prisoners taken by 5
Platoon. *(Mike Moore)*

38. Clearing up on Objective BRASS. CSM Dave Dickson burns Iraqi
vehicles with grenades. *(The Royal Scots)*

39. The prisoners are rounded up and led away. *(The Royal Scots)*

40. Collecting stragglers. Iraqis were coming out of the trenches for some hours after the main surrender. *(G Richardson)*

Because the Warrior had thrown its track before the Company swung round into the FUP it was actually only about ten to fifteen kilometres south of BRASS. The prisoners were almost certainly from that objective originally, probably men who had decided to leave their dug-outs and head in the opposite direction to the incoming Royal Scots' Battle Group attack.

While the Battle Group was swinging round on to BRASS, A2 Echelon continued on the route given to it by Brigade Headquarters, and it was with some surprise therefore that it found itself quite close to the southern part of the objective just as the position was being cleared up. In fact the Battle Group had moved in a wide arc to attack from the rear and A2 Echelon had actually overtaken them.

I remember passing them, looking across and saying to my driver, "Who do you think that is?", and he said, "I think it's ours." They were still finishing off. We were exceptionally wide of the position and it was quite safe for us to move on, otherwise the people at Brigade wouldn't have moved us.

Lieutenant Wendy Smart

Iraqis continued to emerge from their bunkers long after the Battle Group had moved on, particularly from objectives such as BRASS, where the main task was to destroy their means of fighting rather than systematically work from bunker to bunker ensuring that no one was left on the position, a task that would have taken more time than the Battle Group had available during their rapid advance. It was with some consternation therefore that even members of the Echelons found themselves taking prisoners.

I did see someone in a trench, but I think they were more frightened than anything else and therefore they tried to hide as soon as the vehicles came by. It was one of those things. You think, well do you just leave them or do you go and find them, thinking he would eventually have to come out. I didn't want to be the one to run into the trench in all honesty. I'm sure there was another Jock there that would have loved to have done it.

Lieutenant Wendy Smart

I remember one occasion we were all lined up in formation. We were always unloading and loading our vehicle, anything that couldnae' fit anywhere went in the back of ours, you could guarantee it.

We had to completely unload the vehicle and go and collect this mail. This was about five o'clock.

I used to have this wee tape recorder that I bought from one of the garages and I had the Royal Scots' Pipes and Drums and a few other [tapes], and wherever we would go, I had this little Scotland flag where the windshield should have been, and we'd always turn up the music full blast to "The Flower of Scotland" as we drove past everyone just so they'd know we'd be the Jocks.

Off we went, we were told [to] go about sixty Ks that way, it was just like a point. We were told there might be a Chinook coming in dropping off mail and that we'd meet up with other people, but we were the only ones there and there was no sign of nothing!

On the way back I noticed, it must have just caught my eye, it was like a figure, and I was telling Jimmy this, "I'm sure I've seen someone over there", because there was a lot of trenches and it must have been an Iraqi position. There were [only] the two of us, and I'm a bit worried about this. He was saying, "Och, there's nothing there!" I said, "I'm telling you I'm sure there's someone there." So he slowed down where I said to him; it was on the right hand side. I jumped out, and I thought, "My rifle, I'm no going without my rifle." So I picked up my rifle.

It was like trenches in a square, and as I was walking towards it I just seen this figure pop up and he had a pistol! Oh, I was in bits!

I cocked my weapon, and it wouldnae' cock properly. I just [thought], "What'll I do now?" I just took no notice of the guy at this time. I ran round the back of the truck. Jimmy was in the front. He used to put his rifle into a bag to keep all the sand out and it was always behind him while he was driving and of course he was still sitting there. I'm at the back of this waggon banging my rifle to cock it and [the Iraqi] must have thought, "Oh this is the best Britain's got to offer!"

Anyway eventually it did cock, so I went around, well peeked my head round. I'd seen something in his hands and actually he was showing me that it was pointing towards the ground and he put up his hands, but I didn't stay in one place, trying to move about all the time, making sure I was covering him. I said, "Come on, Jimmy, get your rifle out. Come on. What do I do?" He got up to walk towards me and another one popped up and "Oh God", I thought, "I'd better get myself under control", and so I just aimed my rifle at them, told them to come a wee bit closer to me. Those two came close. By that time Jimmy had his rifle and he was covering them, and I actually took a step over towards the trench, which I was very careful about because I had ideas of me going towards this trench to see if there was anyone else in it and, as I was looking over, something happening to me. I tried it as sneaky as possible, and there was someone in there still. I don't know if he was too frightened to come out or not, but he came out, so we told them to take off their jackets, gave them the search.

We put them in the back and I went in the back with them. On the way there, we [had] passed a PoW camp. They were in the back and I thought, "Right, we'll take them to the PoW camp." So off we went. We got lost for a while so we had to backtrack and eventually we got there and while in the back I had my wee cassette with me. While I was covering them, my cassette [had been] hanging on the mirror. I took it off and it was playing "The Flower of Scotland" to them as they were getting searched [to] which Jimmy said, "Put that off you nutter!" I think I just put it on to relax me.

So we took them to the PoW camp and as I was in the back playing my tapes, they were getting quite into it, these Iraqis, and of course being a cheap cassette, I mangled up my tape. I was furious; "My Pipes!" One of them [motioned] to me and I didnae' ken what he's wanting, and one of them started pointing to one of the Iraqis beside him. He was about sixteen, this one and he sort of pointed, and what I thought he was telling me was he's got a weapon there or something. I was banging on [the waggon], "Jimmy, stop, stop!, I think one of these has got a weapon!"

Obviously I did search them before, but I thought I might have forgot something. What it was, I'm sure, was a bit of Hash [Cannabis] or something; it was a cube, and what I think he was trying to do was maybe trying to give us it as a sort of present or something. That's when my tape got mangled up. One of them came quite close to me picked it up, and wound up my tape for me. Fixed it all and put it back in and sort of pointed to see if it was OK if he played it. So he pressed the play button and I was quite surprised that they liked the Pipes. Anyway, we dropped them off at this PoW camp. There was some Captain and we says, "Next time we catch anyone we'll come back; make sure you've got the kettle on!" He says, "Right, I will do."

That afternoon there was another mail collection. On the way back there were about three trucks, [from] English regiments and they wanted to stop to pick up souvenirs from these trenches. Myself and Jimmy, after our experience that morning, said, "If you go, take your weapon and make sure it can cock!" They said, "No, no, this place has been cleared." So out they went and one of them went into this trench and he came running back out. Of course I had my weapon with me because from then on it was [with me] everywhere. He says, "I'm sure there's someone in there", so here we go again!

I went down there and it was like an armoury. There were hundreds of Kalashnikovs on the floor and five Iraqis in that place. Some of them didn't have any trousers on. One of them must have been sixty at least. I think they'd been missed or run away or something and they'd just took shelter.

These English guys would not have them: "They're not going in the back of my truck!" So we took them in ours again.

Since that morning incident, we [had] met up with the chefs and they started giving us their oatmeal biscuits. We had a big cornflakes box full of oatmeal biscuits and wee sucky sweeties. So we started giving them it and they were loving it. The way they were putting it down was like they hadn't been fed. We stopped off at this PoW Camp. "You'se a'bloody'gain!"

Private Mark Morrice

The Plan

After Objective BRASS had been cleared and A2 Echelon had carried out the necessary replenishments, the troops had little time to rest before the Commanding Officer received notification of the next task. Again, the Battle Group had taken its Objective without any casualties, but there was much still to be done, and the Royal Scots had not yet encountered a Republican Guard unit.

Chapter 5

I THINK THERE'S SOME
BASTARD FIRING AT US!

*Then there was a bang bang, and two rounds landed
wide of my vehicle, and my two I/C, Colour Sergeant
Spiers, said, "I think there's some bastard firing at us!"*
Captain Angus McLeod

OBJECTIVE TUNGSTEN
During the afternoon of 26 February Colonel Iain Johnstone warned his Company Commanders that there would
be an Orders Group at 4pm. The Battle Group had been
given another, even larger, Objective – TUNGSTEN – to deal
with, but there was little in the way of detailed information
about its layout.

I went up to get briefed at Brigade Headquarters and they
basically gave us a series of grid references, I think it was about
eight, and said, "There", and reeled off a list which had, I think,
two artillery regiments, one artillery battalion, two tank squadrons, three mechanized infantry companies, two ordinary infantry
companies, and said, "Well, the centre of these things are there.
Go and take them out." The RRF were on the south of us and
they had some other positions as well, not quite as many.
Lt.Colonel Iain Johnstone

26 February 1991, 1700 Been given orders for further deliberate
attacks tonight 20k due E to SL [start line] & then X 8 attack.

Awesome task but most expected to have been attkd by our Arty [artillery] assets.

Lieutenant Guy Richardson

Iain Johnstone demanded and got a further squadron of tanks – A Squadron, 14th/20th Hussars – which he attached to B Company. This meant that the Rifle Companies now each had fourteen Challengers to deal with Iraqi armour as they leap-frogged through the objective. H-hour was to be 8pm so this would be a night attack. So far there had been no casualties in the Battle Group, but would this be the time when the Iraqis started to resist?

I think the biggest battle was initially fear, because we thought it was going to be the hardest one. You almost weigh up in your own mind, you think, "God, you know I've got through those two. This is the third. Is this the unlucky one? Is this going to be more dangerous; more difficult?"

Lieutenant Chris Brannigan

Once again, through no fault of its own, the Battle Group got off to a bad start with the tanks delayed and other traffic cutting them up.

The squadron from 14th/20th was very late and so we were about two hours late by the time we actually set off, because vehicles had run over mines and the things were blowing up and it was all a bit shambly again. Anyway, we moved off. The first half, which was the companies and the tanks, zoomed off. The mortars, RAP, main headquarters and all the administration side of it were in slower vehicles, and they got cut by another massive convoy. Don't know where it was going to, where it had come from, whose it was, but anyway it cut us in two again. I decided to wait, particularly for my mortars and my medical organization, before I went on. So we were actually jolly late by the time we arrived, to meet up with the Recce who'd just finished this contact, and it would appear to us that the enemy were actually going to put up a fight here. This was it, the Recce coming under contact and so on, and a big position.

Lt.Colonel Iain Johnstone

To reach the objective the Battle Group had to cross an oil-pipeline covered by a sand berm. As they went over, the vehicles would be extremely vulnerable to Iraqi counter-attack, especially as the underside of the Warrior was very lightly armoured and would be exposed while they were negotiating the berm. Colonel Johnstone sent the Reconnaissance Platoon forward to look for a suitable place to make an assault crossing.

We'd been sent forward to look for a crossing site, or making sure a crossing site was clear of any enemy, and no mines etc. The CO briefed me at the O Group. Just beforehand, I got a couple of orders, grabbed everyone and we naffed off. We checked the HF [high frequency] was working, and it worked before we left, checked the comms [communications equipment] and off we went. It was about 30 Ks away and in the meantime the comms went down, unbeknown to me. We were getting radio checks, but they stopped working for some reason; although I believe the Rifle Companies could hear me, but I couldn't hear anything back. We ploughed on, must have been well out in front I think, about 30 Ks away from everyone. So I got up near this berm and I thought we'd seen vehicles, three four Ks south; didn't know what they were; weren't interested in them; could have been another Recce platoon for all we knew. Looked up north and about four Ks in front of us, the way we were going, there were some more vehicles up there, they were off slightly north as well, and we saw some troops knocking around on the ground and we thought – well, engineers looking for crossing sites – cause there were said to be other troops in the area, vaguely.

So I selected a final rendezvous, sort of an emergency RV. [I said], "If anything happens from here on in, we come back to this point. You know where you are. If you head due south you'll run into the Battle Group coming up this way." We went forward from there in two halves, my Colour Sergeant going off down the right-hand side, and I went up to the north, and we got virtually on top of this berm. I'm looking out of the top through the Thermal Imager for any sort of mine signs on the ground; couldn't see anything and there was activity in the distance because they were shelling with MLRS from about twenty Ks away, coming right over the top and landing a couple of Ks in front of us. It was at that point someone started firing at us from immediately left of me. I was driving up the road with my Alpha Callsign[1] covering me on the left-hand side. I didn't see the first rounds coming in, just thought it was a bit of noise. Then there was a bang bang, and two rounds landed wide of my vehicle, and my two I/C, Colour Sergeant Spiers, said, "I think there's some bastard firing at us!"

I said to Sergeant MacDonald, "Lay your guns on to those two vehicles up there" – thinking "Blue on Blue; could be a disaster if we shoot our own men up" – "Have you got that Two Two?" "Yeah" "Well fire now!" He started firing and then one of my Corporals said, "There's another vehicle moving behind!" I said, "Well, take that one as well." At that point we all started to fire at it and I said, "Right, let's get off the berm and back towards the RV. Break contact now."

We reversed off there. At that point Colour Sergeant [Spiers'] waggon stopped working; it just stopped dead. Of course they kept firing at his waggon, as we'd left! So Sergeant Copland said, "I'll get him" and he went forward. There was the waggon sitting there, and we kept on firing on the left-hand side and he went forward and got the crew out. I said, "Get that waggon off there!" He went forward; the waggon was still dead; we kept firing; the Colour Sergeant's waggon was still firing up there. I said, "Right, just bale the crew out and leave it!" 'Cause at this point my driver thought he saw T55s just the other side of the berm. We got the crew off and left everything; they got their respirators and rifles and that was about it. No helmets or things, all the kit was inside, and we drove backwards for about 3 Ks and then we couldn't see anything happening, [but we could] still see our vehicle sitting out there, like the dog's bollocks!

I said, "Right, we'd better split it." At this point I sent in a Contact report, saying, "We've had contact; we think we've destroyed two, three vehicles. We're going to split south and north and see if we can find another way around this thing, or see if we can find a crossing site." I reckon we got the wrong grid from the Ops Officer, because we were at the grid the SATNAV said was there, and there was just nothing there. So we split north and south to see if we can find it, try and work round it, and kept a distance off the [berm]. At that point the Colour Sergeant ran into Brigade Headquarters forward, which had arrived about two and a half Ks south, or maybe a bit further. Still no word from Battalion, but they'd heard we'd had contacts and they sent the armour squadron hurrying forward. I picked up Jamie Hewitt. He said, "Right, great. We've got a contact up here. Crossing site? Oh, just cross it, the tanks are going to cross it!" [I said], "Don't worry about the crossing site, just go for it. I've been three or four Ks north and a couple of Ks south. There's nothing else there. You either cross here or that's it." So James Hewitt dragged his whole Squadron across the top of the berm, and they started firing at things across there, as the Battle Group arrived.

That was the "Battle of the Berm" as we called it.

Captain Angus McLeod

I took out one of the vehicles on the left, but then I got a stoppage. But luckily there was another vehicle on the right of our one, and he took out the right one. So I had a stoppage on my first one which was quite embarrassing. [The vehicle I hit] exploded straight away, just burst into flames, I wasn't even sure what round I put in there, I wasn't sure if it was an HE or an armour-piercing round, but I put it straight in and it exploded and it was actually a lot closer than I thought it had been really, and basically lit up the whole place.

After that another couple of vehicles started moving forward and the next thing I heard over the radio was, "Tanks, tanks!" One of our guys went straight into reverse and came back, really really fast. He missed us by about an inch, and you could honestly hear the dirt hitting your vehicle. He'd seen the T55s actually moving towards him. I think that's when one of our vehicles broke down in the middle of a contact, because while this was happening, there was Iraqis all about shooting at us just with small [arms] fire, and I think one of them went straight into reverse. One of our vehicles was actually left in the firing line, ahead of us, so Sergeant Copland went forward with his vehicle, picked up the crew of that vehicle, left the vehicle abandoned, and drove back in the middle of a contact, and there was a lot of fire going down from both sides and there was explosions happening all over the place. Just as the tanks started to come through, everyone started to move back. Our Challengers moved forward and one shot from each and [the T55s] were both out. Took them out with the first round. That's all I could see with my scope anyway; exploded straight away, and then we moved back.

We thought that, OK, if we see a contact, and we report it, that was our job. Our job wasn't really to stand there and fight, but we had to do that that night. It was actually quite lucky that nothing hit us.

Private Nick Williams

Then it was the turn of the Tank Squadrons and Rifle Companies to push forward. The "Order of March" was the Life Guard Squadron followed by A Company, Tactical Headquarters, then 14th/20th Hussars Squadron followed by B Company. Iain Johnstone ordered an assault crossing under cover of a smoke screen provided by the Mortar Platoon.

There was a position located 1100 metres away from the pipeline and we thought that position was going to start engaging the vehicles as we pushed them forward. So Sergeant McLeod, A Company's MFC, had brought the Mortars into action that night, and he had put down a smoke screen, a phosphorous screen, and it lasted for about fifteen, twenty minutes. It was continuous cover while we pushed across the pipeline. It looked brilliant, it really did, just seeing all these rounds going off in the general area. Because we couldnae' purposely identify the position where the actual positions were, Sergeant McLeod just picked a point between the enemy positions and us, just to put a smokescreen down. Bearing in mind you're not supposed to use phosphorous against troops on the ground. It was impressive to see, and again it was good morale for the guys in the actual mortar line, because it felt they were there doing a job. [They] had used Illum on

BRONZE; they had used high explosives on BRASS to a certain extent, and then that was them firing again on the third objective.

Sergeant Peter Fagan

First in were the Life Guards and A Company group which assaulted an artillery position.

The clearest memory I had from TUNGSTEN is how much of a slog it was. I remember, heading towards [it], we drove over cluster bombs or mines or something and I saw a flash in the Image Intensifier. One of the vehicles [had] hit a mine. Quick, check, any damage? No damage. Right, if you hit mines don't worry about it. If it blows you up then you'll let us know about it! The Recce were out in front and they'd reported coming into contact and we could see from where we were, burning vehicles, so we thought this one was going to be quite tough. The Recce had identified BMP tracks; they've got a guy who actually got out, felt in the sand; BMP tracks, which are quite distinctive, and we were quite apprehensive about going on to that one. We went over an obstacle, a sort of sand wall; no doubt there was a pipeline or something underneath it – to get to the objective itself. Once we got on to the objective it was quite easy. We could see so much more in the dark than they ever could. Visibility had improved slightly and there was great illumination from the burning vehicles, and there were exploding tanks and things like that, which put on this great flare of light. You could see all around you, and even though they could see, we were fairly immune to any form of injury, so again it appeared quite easy.

Lieutenant Chris Brannigan

14th/20th and B Company group were to have attacked another nearby artillery position, but there was a danger of them becoming entangled in, or even firing on, the Life Guards and A Company, so Iain Johnstone issued orders for A Company to continue on to the second position. 14th/20th and B Company were then diverted to engage a third, battalion-sized, artillery position, and a Mechanized

Infantry Company. While this was happening, incoming fire was received from the 3rd Royal Regiment of Fusiliers Battle Group, operating further south, fortunately without serious consequences. There was also some sporadic small arms and RPG fire from the Iraqis.

We did receive some small-arms fire back at that stage. There was definitely one guy who was in a bunker, with his weapon, and he was taking on the whole Company, with his AK47. He would give a burst and about every single vehicle in the Company was firing back with chain gun, and we thought we'd got him, but he was firing again, so we had to fire again, but eventually we got him.

There were eight different positions, but it felt as if they were all rolled into one. When you were just carrying on, it just carried on and on. My job was to pick a target and tell my gunner what target to go for. Our waggon never engaged any vehicles. We engaged the bunkers, because the front two platoons had got to take out the vehicles. I took out a few bunkers. You had to be quite close to them to see them to start with, and you'd recognize them mainly by the entrance, because it wasn't as if it was a fighting bunker, it was just a protection bay for them, so it was well dug in, and the entrance was sandbagged and revetted. You could spot the entrance.

Lance Corporal Geoffrey McDermid

After an all-night slog through TUNGSTEN, the Battle Group drew up to form a blocking line to prevent Iraqi forces, thought to be Republican Guard, mounting an attack from the north. While they waited the men took the opportunity to rest and have a bite to eat.

As dawn broke on 27 February the Anti-tank section attached to B Company reported that enemy troops had been seen moving around two large command bunkers, on a nearby ridge, that were thought to have been abandoned. Major Potter therefore ordered the Forward Observation Officer to call down artillery fire on to the position. A

Regimental Fire Mission of twenty-four guns, each firing three rounds as rapidly as possible, and using high and low airburst ammunition, went in. Almost immediately the commander of a US MLRS battery to the north-east of the enemy position called to say that they were receiving incoming artillery fire.

The range and co-ordinates given by the FOO were nowhere near the US position, but a "Check Fire" was called immediately, just in case. Having received news of the loss of two of the neighbouring 3RRF Warriors by a US A10 airstrike, and with the memory of the near engagement of the Dressing Station Five Alpha, The Royal Scots were naturally concerned about another potential "Blue on Blue". It soon became apparent that the Iraqi position was an Observation Post, from which artillery fire was being directed on to the Americans. Some 30mm High Explosive was fired by B Company's Warriors and soon some enemy soldiers appeared carrying white flags. 4 Platoon was sent over to take the surrender, while 6 Platoon provided supporting fire.

As the Warriors approached, the vehicle crews could see a Mobile Rapier vehicle manned by RAF personnel at the other side of the ridge, behind the enemy position, and some of the Iraqis were headed towards it to surrender. It was therefore quite fortunate that the artillery had been called off, and the bunkers engaged with direct fire, or the Rapier section might too have been a victim of so-called "Friendly Fire".

The Platoon quickly debussed, much to the airmen's relief, and rounded up the prisoners while some of the Jocks went over to clear the bunkers.

Our platoon was ordered to go and see what was happening, and take the surrender. When we went over the hill, we actually headed for the area that the prisoners were going to. We could see that they were all sitting down in a big bunch, with these RAF boys, only two or three of them, trying to take the surrender, so I [described] to them as I went over the hill, what was there and [told] them to debus. You give them distance, from five hundred metres down to ten metres, and at the three hundred metre point they open the back door. It goes open at a fair speed. We stopped just short of where the prisoners were and they got out and at that point the Platoon Sergeant took over, designated so many of them to look after the prisoners and the rest of us to go in and take out the position.

I think they were quite glad to see us, the RAF boys, when we came over the hill. We took the prisoners that were there, but also we were told that there was still so many men in some of the bunkers, so the guys went; that was the only time they debussed and used their weapons, was on that position, and they went in and actually cleared the bunkers, using grenade and their weapons.

The guys were working in pairs, going from bunker to bunker, and my job at that time was to support them. Watching what they were doing and looking out for any further positions.

Lance Corporal Geoffrey McDermid

While this was taking place, Iain Johnstone ordered his Company Commanders to get some sleep, so Major Potter handed over to Captain Alex Alderson, his second-in-command.

Lieutenant Dickson's 4 Platoon returned with twenty-four prisoners and B Company's medical team, Lance Corporal Meechan and Private Blake, tended the five Iraqis wounded in the action. Their injuries were logged as follows:

a. Head injury and fractured femur from artillery air bursts. This was treated with 4 First Field Dressings, 3 triangular bandages and an IV drip. The casualty survived.

b. Head injury, cause not known, 1 First Field Dressing. The casualty survived.

c. Left leg injury to thigh and lower leg with entry and exit sites. Caused by artillery. Treated with 6 First Field Dressings, 1 syrette of morphine and an IV drip. The casualty survived.

d. Multiple injuries to head, chest (back and front). Both legs injured, shrapnel wounds to genitalia. Treated with 16 First Field Dressings, 1 syrette of morphine and an IV drip. The casualty survived.

e. Multiple injuries to head, chest, left hand, right leg. Treated with 9 First Field Dressings and an IV drip. Helevac due to severe head injury. Not known if casualty survived.

B Company Diary

One Iraqi was killed, a Major, who died instantly from multiple shrapnel wounds and was buried where he lay. The position was thought to be of Company size with two large Observation Posts. The bunkers contained a wealth of material, including ammunition, mortars, pistols, binoculars, maps and communications equipment. In the trench network were 15–20 scrapes containing ammunition and Anti-Tank Guided Weapons. All this equipment and ammunition was destroyed by the Warriors' 30mm HE fire. Two T55 tanks and two MTLB personnel carriers, on the western part of the position, which had been damaged by artillery fire, were burned out with White Phosphorous grenades. After handing over the prisoners of war, the Platoon Commander returned to his Company, but the Forward Observation Officer and Company Sergeant Major remained behind to destroy a further five Iraqi Landrovers with chain gun and machine-gun fire.

I went across with them. The artillery fire had been effective, because they were all in well dug-in bunkers [and] the rounds had actually gone through these bunkers. We dragged out, I think, about eleven prisoners in all. There was only one of them dead, [but] quite a few [of] them seriously injured, and the guys just did what they could for them. They started applying first aid. The one that was dead was a Major, and we were going through his personal belongings trying to find out if there was any information there that we could use, and the kit he had on was the best of stuff, whereas all the rest of the troops were just conscripts; they were starving; they were scared shitless. This Major had everything. It turned out that he was an Observation Officer. It must have been an OP that they had on that location watching things. So we treated the ones that could be treated, and myself and Sergeant McIver buried the Major. He was pointed towards the sun. We dug a shallow grave and put him in it, and recorded all the details. In fact, when we picked him up, I had his shoulders, Sergeant McIver had his legs and there was nothing at the back of his head at all. His head just sort of disintegrated.

Sergeant Peter Fagan

At about 1.30pm B Company rejoined the Battle Group, which was on 2 hours notice to move. The Battle Group spent the night in the same location, and during the night orders came through to move south to clear an axis to Hafar al Batin, across the Tapline Road to create a Main Supply Route, but this was soon changed. At first light on 28 February the Battle Group moved off for its long-awaited rendezvous with the Republican Guard.

So we stopped there for the night. We were in a minefield of some sort which was inconvenient. But anyway, we stopped there and that night we got orders to go north and south and east and west and people seemed to be changing the plan all of the time. Eventually we got the order that we were to go due east across the Wadi into Kuwait and cut the road leading out of Kuwait in order to destroy the remains of the Republican Guard that we reckon were trapped in there.

Lt.Colonel Iain Johnstone

28 February "G + 4"
0655 moving east into Kuwait to be a stopping line to prevent enemy withdrawal. Going to be about 20 km out of Kuwait City. As we moved through, the many PoWs are giving themselves up all around us in their 100s. Have just given a box of Compo to them. What a nice Guy!

Lieutenant Guy Richardson

As General Schwarzkopf has revealed in his autobiography,[2] General Franks' VII Corps did not make the swift progress that had been anticipated and the situation arose that, although much of the Republican Guard had been destroyed, one more day was needed to complete the job. Meanwhile public opinion, particularly in the United States, was shifting against the apparent shooting-gallery on the Basra Road, and the Arab forces supported by the US Marines had entered Kuwait City. Consequently there was pressure from President Bush to call a cease-fire. So, although all the stated war aims had been achieved, at least part of Saddam Hussein's Republican Guard was able to slip away before meeting the Royal Scots.

Chapter 6

I THINK WE'VE WON!

The CO called an O Group and Norman [Soutar]
walked over to the CO's waggon, and instead of running
back he walked back and I thought, "Bloody Hell!, that
looks as if it's all over." He came back and I said, 'Well,
what's the news?" [He said] "I think we've done it, I
think we've won!"
Lieutenant Chris Brannigan

Early on the morning of 28 February the sun shone as the
Battle Group moved off once again. It was to take up a
blocking position north of Kuwait City, to cut off an enemy
withdrawal. As the waggons crossed the Iraq/Kuwait border
they passed huge columns of Iraqi troops trying to surrender. Unable to accommodate them, the Battle Group
pressed on quickly towards its objective, but at 7.30am it
was stopped some 50 kilometres from Kuwait City. By 8am
news of a provisional cease-fire was coming through.
Although the crews of many of the waggons had tuned into
the BBC World Service and heard the news, the Commanding Officer called his company commanders in for an O
Group to inform them officially. They in turn passed the
information through the chain of command and by mid-
morning it was common knowledge throughout the Battle
Group.

28 Feb. "G + 4" – 0800 Cease-fire just came into effect. 1015 the
sun has come out for the first time in 5 days (as have the flies) and

I have just seen some birds. God may be trying to tell us something!

Lieutenant Guy Richardson

Myself and Corporal Campbell, I think we were among the last to know. We were out, (surprise, surprise!). We'd come back from a mail [run] and we [saw] all these Shermulies. It was like fireworks and I was thinking, "That's coming from our camp. What's happening?" And we'd stopped off at this place, must have been only about a mile away, it was where the post room itself was, one of these field post rooms, and they were out there, [saying] "It's actually finished!"

Private Mark Morrice

After the cease-fire had been announced, it was time to take stock of the situation and deal with the fatigue and the conflicting emotions engendered by such a rapid and successful campaign. Although the men could have fought on, everyone was very tired, some even beyond sleep.

On the day of the cease-fire the weather was good. By the time we'd come to a halt a sandstorm had blown up and I had an AK47 that we all thought we were going to be able to get back, and I was desultorily cleaning it. I was physically shattered, but my mind had not yet stopped. I was not able to go to sleep. It took two or three days to come down off that heightened sense of alertness that you get into, even when you are that tired.

Lieutenant Alastair Stobie

Many of the officers and men had mixed feelings. On the one hand they had taken part in a war and had survived, but on the other their combat had been brief and remote. Some felt that, while they were glad to be alive, they had not really engaged the enemy the way infantry should.

Contact in my eyes or how I had envisaged it was company vehicles being taken out, us seeing our targets, hitting targets we'd seen clearly and getting on the ground and mixing it. Which is what we were all about. Although we were armoured, we weren't tankies, we weren't the cavalry. We are infantry, although *armoured* infantry, and at the end of the day, what the job is is to get out on the ground with a rifle and bayonet and kill people that you can see; individuals rather than targets. So I didn't feel that we'd been in a contact, although we had.

2nd Lieutenant Roger Walker

Even after the cease-fire, there was one last task to do. An Iraqi re-broadcast station was transmitting messages in the forlorn hope that it might encourage the troops to fight on, so A Company and the Life Guards were sent out to silence it.

We went off on a great charge across the desert, with the Life Guard Squadron, to take them out, and that was the day after the cease-fire. This broadcasting station was still passing out messages encouraging people to fight, so the orders came through to go and destroy that and we raced off across the desert with two choppers and all that sort of kit. When we got there we found some Egyptians had captured the people responsible, who weren't any part of a signals unit; they were almost certainly part of the Iraqi Special Forces and they were subjected to a quick interrogation which proved fairly fruitless. That really was our last task.

Lieutenant Chris Brannigan

A Company got the word to go back into Iraq to look for a radio station, what they thought was a radio station. I went back to A Company and got to an RMP checkpoint, and there's the Iraqis, they didn't have any idea where it was, they'd actually walked up to this checkpoint, twenty or thirty kilometres, and they were trying to walk back to Baghdad. They hadn't a clue where they were, they were from positions on the Saudi/Iraq border. They looked in better condition; they'd had the chance to keep themselves better, which made us all think they were Republican Guard. Whether they were or not I don't know. We had very little chance to question them freely, because there [were] two

Egyptian LOs [Liaison Officers] at the checkpoint and again, it's the old Arab thing, "My Brother" and all the rest of it, and they were very concerned that the Brits were coming back and picking on Arabs again.

Captain Dermot Fulton

Some of the Jocks had spent nearly the entire war in the dark, stuffy and claustrophobic confines of the back of a Warrior, surrounded by ammunition, and being driven into tremendous fire-fights, while entirely reliant on the men in the turret giving them information on the situation. It was important therefore for everyone to be made aware of what they had taken part in and what the Royal Scots Battle Group had achieved.

Iain Johnstone very seldom told me what to say in my sermons. Very seldom had he ever suggested anything, but he was quite keen that I would emphasize the fact that we'd done a real job. He was concerned that Jocks of all ranks might think, "I didn't do anything. I've been out there. I've come home and I didn't do a thing!", and wanted everyone to know that they were all vital links in a military unit that had done a superb job, and so we worked quite hard on that, and in Church we'd repeat that.

Major Stephen Blakey

This was the start of a period of adjustment, of getting the men back to normality, so that there would be no problem later. It was fortunate, in one sense, that there was a wait of over a month before the men could go home. It gave them time to unwind, to come down off the adrenalin high that they had experienced.

After the Gulf we went through a period where we tried to get back to a normal level. We did a lot of sport. We set up recreational units where you could go and play this and play that. They could meet [and] basically they could discuss what they'd seen, what they'd done and what could have happened. What might have happened, that type of thing. We found that it brought them down, so by the time they [got home] they'd forgotten the hard bit, the actual fighting bit.

Sergeant Tom Gorrian

There was a lot of just allowing people to unwind and relax and so on, and yet with soldiers you can't allow them to do it too long. You need to keep people busy and active and so on, so there was a certain amount of on-going training. But it was a great month. We ran a library and all the parcels were coming through, so I used to distribute those. It was a good time, it was a happy time, we *almost* definitely weren't going to war again and you were away from home. It was a nice setting; the sand was clean; the bank manager wasn't writing toyou. It was a very carefree month with that lingering question about how long is this going to go on for, but with the knowledge that actually on the whole the danger was over. The pressure was off and you could just mellow out.

Major Stephen Blakey

On Sunday 3 March the cease-fire was formally ratified. Meanwhile the Royal Scots, although at a slightly lower level of preparedness, were still carrying live ammunition and keeping their vehicles in good running order. At about 10am tragedy struck. Private Tom Haggerty of A Company was carrying out routine maintenance on his waggon. He was using a torque wrench to make some adjustments to a wheel. It was a warm morning and he had taken off his webbing. It lay on the sand, within reach, and close to the vehicle. Suddenly the unthinkable happened. The heavy torque wrench slipped off the vehicle wheel and the head of it struck his webbing apparently causing a grenade to detonate, which in turn must have set off the rest of the ammunition he had been carrying, causing a massive explosion. Haggerty was killed instantly. His loss was a devastating blow to the entire Battalion, but it was fortunate for his comrades that he had taken the full force of the blast, for he had saved them from serious injury or even death.

The men who were in the Company area heard the explosion and saw a plume of smoke. One of the first on the scene was the Warrior Captain, Chris Brannigan, but Haggerty's Section Commander said, "It's too late, Boss, he's dead."

Private Pearson, the section's gunner, who was up on the turret, cleaning the gun, was blown off the vehicle by the force of the explosion, but was unhurt.

The actual blast threw me off the vehicle. Soon as the explosion went off, I picked myself up and it was a quick look around to see if anyone's missing, so we went under the tarpaulin and me and the commander, Sandy Mack, pulled him out.

Private Peter Pearson

At first it was thought that Haggerty had stepped on an enemy mine, but an investigation soon revealed the apparent cause of the explosion.

It was a torque wrench in fact which is very much heavier than what you'd think of as your average spanner. He was torquing up wheel nuts on the vehicle during routine vehicle maintenance. We had these little day sacks, and they were full, one with medical kit and the other one with spare ammunition, including five CLAW grenades, this rifle-launched Close Assault Weapon, five white phosphorous grenades, five L2 Grenades and some small arms ammunition. Nobody actually saw this happen, but this was the considered opinion of the Ammunition Technical Officer who came round. [Haggerty] slipped with the torque wrench, which is easy to do, but hit the top of one of these CLAW grenades with such force that the concussion detonated the grenade, which then sympathetically detonated the remainder. The reason that the Ammunition Technical Officer could be so accurate about that was that the torque wrench was splayed at the head and this is a big heavy piece of equipment. Had it not been at the point of the explosion it would not have splayed like that.

It hit the Company very hard indeed. We had expected to take a lot of casualties, and hadn't. We then thought we were all through it, and he genuinely was one of the most remarkable characters in the battalion. He'd just previously come back from Northern Ireland. He'd volunteered to spend six months there with the Gordon Highlanders. He was lively, he was respected and liked by his superiors and subordinates alike. Some soldiers are very quiet, keep themselves to themselves, and others are real characters, and he was real character. It hit everybody really badly that this had happened, and it seemed such a tragedy that it happened when it did. The whole Battalion said prayers for him that morning and his family.

Captain Robert Bruce

Because it was no longer necessary to carry the full combat load, and in order to prevent further accidents, the following day the men handed in their grenades and strict controls were imposed on those carrying live ammunition. But there were apparently other near misses and searching every pocket, container and every corner of every vehicle became a necessity.

We used to have this wee bonfire and we used to get the crates of these non-alcoholic beverages and we'd all sit down, quite a few of us, and people used to come from A2 Echelon to the actual wee thing, and we'd gossip and have a wee chat, and a wee joke, a wee sip of the [non-alcoholic] beer. We just used to speak about, well, normal squaddie things I suppose which was quite a good laugh and try and play a few silly games like I Spy, in the desert, which was totally hopeless!

I remember, it was not long after Tam Haggerty, the incident with him, in fact it was the following day, we were sitting round this little fire and we'd got called away. Now everyone was handing in their ammo that day before and this day, and someone had this . . . it was like a potato sack and there was a pair of desert combats in it, and he's shoved that in the fire and unknown to any of us there was a grenade in it! As we were walking away the grenade went off. The speed of the Medics and all that, over there, was just so quick. Of course they knew roughly who stayed in that little tent in the area where it was. I was too busy just laying down on the ground! I think I was out of the range anyway. But lucky enough it all blew that way instead of that way! A couple of minutes before that there must have been about six or seven people around the fire.

Private Mark Morrice

Gradually the strictly imposed discipline of routine and dress was relaxed. First to go was the Combat Body Armour, and ultimately the men's shirts. At last they could relax, sunbathe and look forward to being reunited with their families.

To fill the days, training cadres were organized to upgrade the men's personal skills and improve their prospects of promotion, and ranges were set up to fire off the spare ammunition.

Friday March 22 1991 – Up early and left for the ranges at 0730 after picking up ammo. Started firing at c.1030. 51mm, L2, White Phos, CLAW and 9mm. I basically set up ranges and gave arcs. Stobes [Lt.Stobie] stayed on safety net. Chased Kuwaiti soldiers off range, whacky races trying to catch them. When I did we all had to shake hands and hug as if I had liberated Kuwait single-handedly.

2nd Lieutenant Roger Walker

The Padre was on hand to talk to any of the men who had difficulty in making the rapid adjustment from war to peace, and he was pleased to find that the experience of going to war had led some men to religion.

There were a certain number of individuals who quite openly became Christians. During the month at the end we sat in the same spot of sand for four weeks. I ran, I suppose, a sort of Confirmation Class and we had about eight people come to that. There were those who quite openly made conversions; but a lot, underneath it, were much happier talking about God.

Major Stephen Blakey

I think we've won!

Although the Battle Group was in Kuwait, few of the men
had the opportunity to visit Kuwait City to see the devas-
tation caused by the Iraqi invaders. Those that did were
shattered by the sights and by the smell. Like all the
Coalition troops, they were welcomed as liberators wherever they went.

We went towards Kuwait City, and on the road was traffic on
each side and right down the middle it was just all burnt-out
vehicles. When me and Jimmy were driving through it, it was like
you could smell the bodies. There were still bodies in certain
vehicles; we'd seen them taking out the bodies. There were still a
few fights, not much, the Americans had really done the business,
but you could hear the wee shots just in the distance. But I'll
never forget that smell. We both looked at one another and the
smell was just . . . I've not smelt anything like it. It was just . . .
I've never smelt burning flesh but that smell, you knew it was
something like that.
      You had all these small children and the women on the side of
the road, running up obviously to try and wave at you and the
women were waggling their tongues or whatever they do,[1] and we
were looking at the buildings, and the majority of the buildings
were just covered with flags. I remember one, it was like a block
of flats and there was a flag that just covered the whole building.
The garages had been raided and the few people taking advantage
of the new cars that they knew they could get into and drive
away. There was a lot of actual Kuwaiti people who were going
through shops that had been looted trying to get things for
themselves. We had kept quite a lot of sweeties and were flinging
them at the kids. Where the mail was collected was Kuwait
Airport itself and that was some sight.

Private Mark Morrice

At last the Royals received the news that they were going
home. The troops in the armoured vehicles were taken by
bus to the airport at Dahran, but those with wheeled
vehicles had to make the return journey from Kuwait to
Saudi Arabia by road.

Wednesday 3 April 1991 – The last day. Rose 0600 moved to square at 8. Arrived at Dahran. Flew by Jumbo jet to Hanover, arrived at 2045. Back to Werl reception. It's great to be home.

Corporal Derek Notman

On one of the flights from Saudi Arabia there was some unexpected in-flight entertainment when one of the stewardesses looked strangely familiar to some of the men as they were woken up by the sound of hysterical laughter.

During the flight he [Private Alastair Howie] was talking away to the air hostess, and she seemed quite chirpy, she said, "How about a set of your combats?" He says, "Well, I've only got one pair, those I've got on." [She said] "Well, you get into my kit and I'll get into your kit." He was one of the lads, out for laugh so [he said] "Nae probs!" They were away to the stern, away for about half an hour or so, and he came back. "Anyone want coffee?" he said in a female voice. I think half the guys were actually sleeping at the time but I think they all got woken up by the amount of laughter that was going on at the time. I think that was when we actually realized that it was all over.

Private John Drain

The return to Werl was well organized and Iain Johnstone had fought hard for permission to get the men back to Scotland, on leave, within hours of their arrival in Germany.

All the Sergeant Majors were sent back first. The plan was to get everyone on leave within twenty-four hours. So, it was great. We were gone. We were on our way. From Kuwait, we had our final breakfast there, got on to the trucks to the forward air base where there was a Herc waiting for us and that was run by the RAF ground-crews; they were very very good; everything was ready for us; we arrived there and they were ready to process us. The Herc came in, I don't know what his total load was supposed to be; we were piled up to the roof. We flew off and we arrived, got back to Blackadder Camp. We were stuck in there for about a couple of days, which was really annoying, because by then

I think we've won!

Blackadder Camp was like a tip, stinking. People were beginning to get a bit touchy about it. We then got our flight timings, got on our flight and, Oh, it couldn't have been better; we were in the First Class, treated like kings. It was excellent. Unfortunately the flight we got was an Arab flight so there was no drink on it! But it was no big deal. We were going home. We got to the other end, the Piper was there, reception committee and all the rest of it. We then got back to the Camp and there was yellow ribbons from the Camp gate all the way up to the Gymnasium, and there was a party there for us when we got there, the wives were there, my daughter, my son-in-law, it was fantastic.

WO2 Dave Dickson

When the main body of the Royals arrived, they were not allowed out of camp that night, but few if any wanted to go, they were all intent on packing their kit and getting away to their flights home, and, for many, an emotional reunion with their families.

Colonel Johnstone knew basically what he had on his hands was a time bomb. All it'd have took was for a couple of the guys to get really a wee bit drunk on the bevy. Before you knew it, the whole battalion would have been down the town, and at the end of the day I don't think the public relations with Germany would have been very good. So it was off the buses, meet the families, grab your tackle, head to the lines, everybody on parade. OK, this is when your flight times are. OK, you're up at two o'clock in the morning, we're flying out. Within twenty-four hours we were back in Edinburgh.

Private John Drain

It was well organized when we came back, because we got paid right away, all the credits we had from the German banks. The German bank was actually in the camp, so it was quite good, I was quite impressed with that. Everyone got away and when we got back to Edinburgh, it was just out of this world.

Private Paul Hosie

I was married but I was unaccompanied. I suppose it was the same for a lot of the single guys. I suppose because the married men had their wives there, the majority of them, and it felt like they were getting this great welcome. We went into the Gym and there was a couple of beers; obviously you tried to sneak as many beers as possible, sandwiches etc.

I decided right, I think I'll go and get myself settled down and get ready to go home. So I went to see Sergeant Major Cochrane; he'd arrived back before us. He told us to come back at a certain time and he'd let us know about our flights. I put in for Luton instead of Edinburgh, because my family lived down in Wales at that time, so Luton's a lot closer. Lucky enough my flight came, I only had to wait maybe ten or eleven hours before I was actually on the move for my flight, so I was quite pleased about that. The NAAFI was open and so we went down there, got a little bit drunk. We hardly got any sleep that night at all because we were all up chattering.

The actual flight itself, which was quite good, landed in Luton and I remember being one of the first off, and I was walking through. There was quite a few other Jocks with me and I was looking about and all I could hear was this scream, I thought, "Oh aye", and there she was, my Mother, with this big huge yellow ribbon, all wrapped around herself saying, "Welcome Home Son". My younger brother was there and my Dad had the camera with him.

Of course my wife was there as well. My Mum had told my wife, "When he comes off I'll let you see him first, 'cause you're his wife", but that just went straight out the window. Soon as she'd seen me my Ma was off, she was after me. I just dropped my bags and I ran, 'cause I know what my Mum's like when she gets going, I probably would have been licked to death!

Private Mark Morrice

Mum came and burst out greeting,[2] and I burst out crying myself and then got in the car, followed up, me and my brother and my Dad. We took a couple of boys back, as well, so we came back with their mum and dad as well. When I got back to my house there was flags in the house and "Welcome Home Paul" all in the house. I just carried my bags over. I just walked up to the house, and my brother [said], "Well go in then, go in then!" "What do you mean, go in then?" I said, "I've no got the key." He goes, "No, it's open" and just as he opened it, someone shut the living room door and of course that's where all my relations were. So there and then, I went straight into the kitchen, I had some desert combats that I wanted to bring back, and I put my desert combats on and I went into the living room and that's where all my aunties and uncles, my granny, were all there, and that was me. The party started about half past seven, the time we got home. I lasted; I started to talk a load of rubbish, and ended up collapsing in a ball in the corner. That was at one o'clock.

Private Paul Hosie

After I got back from the whole conflict a lot of [my friends] didn't want to talk, they were embarrassed. I didn't think I had done anything remarkable, but a lot of them just didn't want to talk to me about it. They didn't want to approach me, didn't want to ask how we'd done or anything, just avoided the situation completely.

Private Nick Williams

After a well-earned leave the Battalion began to reassemble at Werl to prepare for its move to Inverness, and on 2 June a Drumhead service of thanksgiving was held. During the Service Private Tom Haggerty was remembered. The Battalion was represented at the Welcome Home parades, both in New York and London. On 10 June, 1991, in Manhattan, 4.7 million people crammed into two miles to give a ticker-tape welcome to the Gulf War heroes. The British contingent, led by General Sir Peter de la Billière, included Lance Corporal Lamont and Privates Cook, Littlewood, Latimer, Boyd and Derbyshire of the Royal Scots. They were led by Alastair Stobie, Commander of 5 Platoon in the Gulf, who had recently been promoted to Captain. He proudly carried the Union Jack as he marched along Broadway dressed in desert combats and glengarry, flanked by representatives of the other British services.

We were sitting in a bar, where else, drinking free beer, why not; watching the first elements of the US contingents wading their way up 5th Avenue. It was then that I realized quite what I was involved in. The biggest ticker-tape parade that New York had ever hosted, and the previous ones had not been exactly small.

The television pictures looked appalling. It was barely possible to make out the troops through the vast quantities of ticker tape, computer paper and the contents of litter bins being emptied from the financial centres stretching inexorably upwards all around us. The noise was deafening even from where we were some 500 metres away from 5th Avenue.

They finally managed to turf us out of the bars, and form us up on Bridge Street which is at right-angles to 5th Avenue in the very south of Manhattan Island, with the promise that we would be stepping off shortly. Two hours later we finally did step off into the howling din.

If, as we stood and waited, we had our picture taken once, we had it taken a thousand times. When we finally stepped out into the maelstrom of 5th Avenue, the noise was deafening, the atmosphere electric. By the time we passed as the last of the foreign contingents, some ten thousand troops had already been up the route. This had not dented the crowd's enthusiasm one little bit. At particular bottle-necks it was impossible to hear yourself think, let alone hear the bass drum. This incredible party continued for a mile and a half past "Stormin" Norman Schwarz-kopf amongst other dignitaries. Then suddenly it was all over and the "Mother of all Parties" began. It was almost impossible to buy yourself a beer. In fact I did not all night!

Captain Alastair Stobie

The London Welcome Home Parade took place on 21 June, and a party of eight from the Battalion represented The Royal Scots and made up the total Scottish contingent of the marching half-company of 4 Brigade. Preparations started in Sennelager Training Centre with groups of soldiers marching around the grounds giving the occasional "Eyes Left" to confused gardeners. The contingent was then flown to London, and continued training in Hounslow

41. Major John Potter gives the victory salute as The Royal Scots Battle Group enters Kuwait, 27 February, 1991. (*Mike Moore*)

42. Wrecked Iraqi vehicles litter the desert. (*R Walker*)

43. The war is over! Reg Brindley grins at the camera, 28 February, 1991. *(R Brindley)*

44. Comparison between the Warrior (left) and an Iraqi T55 (right). *(G Richardson)*

45. An aerial view of the Basra Road. *(W Smart)*

46. A victory photograph in front of the CO's Warrior: Iain Johnstone (centre) flanked by his Company

Barracks, where they were put through their paces by the Garrison Sergeant Major, so that they could cover the precise distance of the official route in the allotted time. The dress rehearsal took place at midnight along the actual route, on Wednesday the 19th, to the surprise and appreciation of some late-night stragglers as they made their way home from pubs and restaurants. The Parade itself began at midday on Friday the 21st with a helicopter fly-past. The route ran from the Old Artillery Ground near Finsbury Square, past the Mansion House, where HM The Queen took the salute, and ended at the Guildhall where a buffet reception awaited the participants.

On 6 November, 1991, Majors Potter and Soutar and Private Gow attended the investiture at Buckingham Palace, where they received their gallantry awards from HM The Queen.

A Gulf War Medal Parade took place at Fort George, Inverness, on 13 February, 1992. HRH The Princess Royal, Colonel-in-Chief of the Royal Scots, presented Gulf Medals to a representative party from the Battalion, and presented Mention in Despatches Certificates to Captain McLeod, Sergeant Copland and Lance Corporal Gibb. The parade was also attended by Major Bryan Johnston, who braved the cold weather, despite some discomfort from his wounds; by Mike Moore, the photographer from *Today* newspaper who had accompanied the Battle Group into action; and by Tom Haggerty's parents. The latter proudly received their late son's Northern Ireland and Gulf medals from the Princess Royal.

As far as Iain Johnstone was concerned, this parade marked the end of an era.

You can't look backwards all the time. There has to be a certain point when you have got to start looking to the future. The Parade marked the end of the Gulf era for us and a very fitting end it is, but we have new challenges to face. The Gulf was such an enormous operation. It was something that involved us in a way that I don't think anything else has before, and probably won't again.

We learned a lot about ourselves, as did our families. Now is the time to put it behind us, consolidate the lessons we learned and go forward.

Lt.Colonel Iain Johnstone

Epilogue

THE MOTHER OF ALL BATTLES

"When the battle becomes a comprehensive one with all types of weapons, the deaths on the allied side will be increased with God's help. When the deaths and the dead mount on them, the infidels will leave and the flag of Alluhu Akbar will fly over the Mother of all Battles."
Saddam Hussein, Baghdad Radio, 20 January, 1991

Among the soldiers I interviewed during my research for this book, the generally held opinion was that the Coalition should have pressed on to Baghdad and removed Saddam Hussein from power. Although his political, if not his physical, demise would no doubt have caused great rejoicing, the fact remains that the Coalition achieved all that was asked of it by the Kuwaiti and Saudi Arabian governments. The Iraqi forces were ejected from Kuwait, Kuwaiti sovereignty was restored and, importantly, this was all achieved without upsetting the status quo in the region. From a purely western point of view, the reduction of Saddam Hussein's massive arsenal was a high priority. It was also better to achieve this while fighting to liberate Kuwait than to risk the horrifying possibility of Iraq developing, or purchasing, nuclear weapons or inter-continental ballistic missiles capable of reaching a European or American city.

It is somehow ironic that at the time of writing this book, Saddam Hussein is still clinging to power in Iraq, whereas Margaret Thatcher, British Prime Minister at the time of the

Iraqi invasion of Kuwait, and George Bush, President of the United States during the entire conflict, have both been voted out of office (in Thatcher's case, by her own colleagues). Indeed, even the military leaders, Generals Schwarzkopf and de la Billière, have now retired and, for a time, it seemed as though The Royal Scots, Britain's oldest infantry regiment, would cease to be.

When he took his Battalion to war, Iain Johnstone was conscious that he was engaged in a dual conflict. The obvious one was the destruction of the Iraqi forces his Battle Group was to meet. This, as you have seen, The Royal Scots did without any real problems. However, Colonel Johnstone was also fighting for his Regiment's survival. For under the Ministry of Defence's Options for Change, no unit, not even the senior infantry regiment in the British Army, was safe.

During the Royal Scots' service in the Gulf, Iain Johnstone took great pains to project just the right profile for his men, conveying their fearsome but enviable reputation to the journalists, and also making sure that everyone measured up to the high standard he had set. Just before the start of the ground war he wrote to Colonel R. S. B. Watson, OBE, at HQ Scottish Division:

I have but one aim: to win the war in order to ensure my Regiment's survival!! My press efforts and our best efforts will be that aim. It's an exciting time and I wouldn't miss it for the world. I must be the envy of almost every Battalion Commander – great officers, the best soldiers, new kit that works, up to strength with a message from HRH [The Princess Royal] in the pocket, in the Queen's thoughts and have just had a letter from my wife! What could be better!

But, soon after their return from war the Royals were greeted with devastating news. On 23 July, 1991, the announcement was made that the Royal Scots would have to amalgamate with the King's Own Scottish Borderers. Soon after this, RHQ received a communication from Army HQ Scotland. Was it a reprieve? No, it was a notice of a revised procedure for ordering lavatory paper!

News of the amalgamation under Options for Change was broken two days before Parliament rose for the summer recess, perhaps in the hope that the controversy would have been forgotten by October when both houses reassembled, and any campaigns mounted to overturn these decisions would have lost momentum.

However, instead the Royal Scots prepared themselves for their own "Mother of all Battles" with a massive campaign. Despite a march to Westminster, and Petitions handed in at the Houses of Parliament, followed by pressure in Parliament after the reassembly in October, it seemed as though the amalgamation would go ahead. Reluctantly a new name was chosen for the amalgamated unit, together with details of dress and insignia, with much thought given to salvaging the traditions of both regiments.

Ultimately, the deployment of British troops to Bosnia emphasized what the Ministry of Defence had been reluctant to admit in that the Army was stretched to breaking point and to reduce it was a nonsense. At last, the government saw reason and on 3 February, 1993, the announcement was made that The Royal Scots were to be saved.

Of the officers and men who served with the Battalion in the Gulf, about half have now left the Army, some of them having taken voluntary redundancy under the provisions of Options for Change. Among those that are still serving, many have been promoted. Iain Johnstone, now a Brigadier, has recently taken command of the British Forces in Belize. After handing over the Royals to Lieutenant Colonel Bill Sylvester in May, 1992, he was looking forward to a tour of duty in the United States on the staff of his Gulf War Corps Commander, General Franks. However, a victim of his own success, Iain Johnstone was sent at short notice to Zagreb, with the rank of Colonel, as Chief of Staff of the European Commission Monitoring Mission. Dressed entirely in neutral white, so that they would be visible, their job there was, as Colonel Johnstone put it, "negotiating the unnegotiable with the insane". Then followed a three-month Higher Command Staff Course at Camberley before his current assignment.

Of the Company Commanders, Norman Soutar and Bryan Johnston have now left the Army, and John Potter has been promoted to Lieutenant Colonel and has command of a battalion of The Royal Irish Regiment. Captain James Stevenson, who took over Fire Support Company when Bryan Johnston was wounded, has been selected to attend Staff College.

The Battalion, brought up to strength with fresh intakes from the regimental depot and reinforced by an airborne artillery regiment, has undergone another period of intense training and yet another change in Order of Battle, during which the Fire Support Company was temporarily disbanded, and has just completed a six-month tour in Northern Ireland.

Private Vincent Stott, now old enough to serve there, was among the Royals carrying out the dangerous task of supporting the Royal Ulster Constabulary in South Armagh. During this time there were several close shaves, culminating in the death of 26-year-old Corporal Lawrence Dickson. Married and the father of an eighteen-month-old daughter, he was murdered by an IRA sniper on St Patrick's Day, 17 March, 1993.

After the war Second Lieutenant Roger Walker went out into the desert and expressed his feelings in verse. It was the first, and very probably the only, poem he would ever write:

> The sand, the moon, a shooting star
> The Plough, our friend from lands afar
> Showing us the way home.

> The sky so many shades of blue and grey,
> The moon ruling night as the sun ruled the day.
> On the horizon a clear orange haze
> With plumes of smoke drifting into the greys.
> Such a sorry land.

> The last post sounds the closing of the day
> Our last in the desert which we never made our home.
> We leave it to the Arabs, to fight over these lands
> Of Wadis, Sabka sea and sands.

> We did not want it, it was never our mission
> To capture and hold territorial position.
> To clear and kill, destroy bunkers and tanks
> Those were the orders of General Franks.

> Close with the enemy, bayonet and maim.
> That's what we trained for, that was our aim.
> That's why we came.
> Or so we thought at the time.

> They surrendered in scores,
> No stomach for a fight,
> Bombarded for days,
> Assaulted that night.

The speed we advanced, it could not be true.
'Those infidel white men have powerful Ju-Ju.'
The fear on their faces was so clear to see
'Get yer hands on yer heed! Get doon on yer knee!'
Our Arabic was poor but they still understood,
Facing Warrior and bayonet anyone would.

Then came the cease-fire,
We were travelling at speed
Towards Kuwait City where we heard of the greed
And destruction and torture of innocent folk
By the enemy troops who were now in retreat.

Withdrawing North, the Republican Guard,
We were to destroy, it would not have been hard
As had been proved already, with superior tanks
And air supremacy, for that we gave thanks.
Cut off their routes to the Basra Pocket.
The evil of Saddam, we could finally stop it.

The grey suits in Whitehall and Capitol Hill
Had succumbed to the pressure (lacked the political will)
Of the peace campaigners and the public at large.
'Remember Vietnam and the high body count.'
'Ground all the planes. Get the troops to dismount.'

I felt no elation. I only felt cheated
Here was our chance to see Saddam defeated.
Now our prey was master again
They were now slaying when they should have been slain.
Inflicting torture and murder and rape,
Phosphorus bombs and Napalm.

How they cried when a few civilians
Were killed in the destruction of a military bunker
Placed there to shield, or for political gain
And sure enough the left fell for Hussein.

But now they continue to murder their own.
They gassed them before, and they will do it again.
Where are the 'Humanitarians' now!

And the orange glow on the horizon still burns
And we go home.

Roger Walker

NOTES

1. The former Ottoman Empire was divided up into vilayets or provinces.
2. On 16 May, 1916, an agreement between Sir Mark Sykes (on behalf of the British Government) and Georges Picot (on behalf of the French), subsequently called the Sykes Picot Agreement, provided for the division and colonization of the Ottoman Empire between Britain and France after the war, despite assurances made by Lawrence of Arabia in his efforts to persuade the Arabs to revolt against Turkish rule in 1916. Readers should also be aware of the Balfour Declaration, a communication made on 2 November, 1917 by A. J. Balfour, British Foreign Secretary, to Lord Rothschild, a leader of Zionism, declaring British support for the establishment of a Jewish national home in Palestine.
3. Major-General Sir Percy Cox (1864–1937) was Chief

Political Officer, Indian Expeditionary Force 'D', 1914–1918; Acting British Minister to Persia, 1918–1920 and High Commissioner in Mesopotamia 1920–1923.

Chapter 1 (pp 11–37)

1. The Boyd Cycle was named after a study of air-to-air combat during the Korean War, made by Colonel John Boyd of the US Air Force. He concluded that the faster an airman or soldier could make the transition through the cycle from observation to appreciation, to decision, to action, the more likely he was to win the battle by taking the initiative away from his enemy.
2. The Staffords were the Armoured Infantry Battalion attached to 7 Brigade.
3. On 11 March, 1972, three young soldiers, two of them under 18, were abducted from a pub and murdered. The bodies were recovered in a ditch in Ligoniel, on the outskirts of Belfast. Consequently, the Ministry of Defence announced that soldiers under 18 would not serve in Northern Ireland.

Chapter 2 (pp 38–78)

1. Blackadder Camp was named after the central character in a BBC TV series of the same name.
2. Boogie box was the popular term within the Battalion for a personal stereo.
3. Illness was a serious problem for the Expeditionary Force in Mesopotamia during the First World War, causing nearly half of the estimated 28,000 deaths.
4. The Royal Scots left a rear party at Werl, including the Unit Families Officer, Captain Mick Low, who was in constant contact with Lieutenant Bill Sutherland in B2 Echelon, thereby ensuring that the families were

updated and did not have to rely on rumour and press speculation.

5. NBC suit: A fabric oversuit with a hood, in which the lining was impregnated with charcoal to protect the wearer against nuclear, biological and chemical weapons. It was worn with cotton gloves and rubber overgloves and rubber overboots, and a respirator.

6. This translation, which does not coincide with any of the leaflets catalogued by The Psywar Society, was copied into his note book by Lieutenant Colin Dougan during an intelligence briefing in the Gulf.

7. Named after their manufacturer, Shermulies were hand-held mini-flares rather like fireworks.

8. Each soldier was issued with an auto-inject syrette of morphine for use if he was wounded. The tip of the syrette was held against the leg and a hypodermic needle plunged through the soldier's clothing if the device was activated.

9. Heat-seeking weapons could be diverted if a heat source such as a burning oil drum was positioned close to the vehicle at which the missile was aimed.

10. The objectives in the ground war were named after metals such as BRONZE, BRASS and TUNGSTEN.

Chapter 3 (pp 79–100)

1. The Iraqi Airforce was never a force to be reckoned with. Many aircraft were destroyed by low-level attacks on the hardened aircraft shelters, and the runways were cratered by runway denial bombs to prevent those that survived from taking off. The few Iraqi aircraft that took to the air were either destroyed in air-to-air combat or fled to Iran where they were impounded. However, as the Coalition forces crossed into Iraq there was some concern that Saddam Hussein had saved some

of his airforce for an aerial attack with chemical weapons.

2. For some reason the communications system in the Commanding Officer's Warrior kept getting stuck in the 'Send' mode, which made it very difficult for him to receive orders from Brigade. Although it was inspected several times by the Battle Group REME technicians, and repaired, the actual problem causing this malfunction was never traced.

3. The bomblets were from the Multi-Launch Rocket System projectile which scattered more than 7000 'sub munitions' of which 5 to 10 percent failed to explode on impact with the soft desert sand.

4. To 'Echelon' through is military parlance for one unit passing through another.

5. Infra Red Image Intensification sights could be used at night to enhance vision. They made use of what little ambient light there was, but could be blinded by red lights such as were on the rear of each vehicle.

6. Thermal Imaging picked up the 'heat signature' of a vehicle and transmitted it as a glowing image, but it could not provide an accurate profile from which an enemy vehicle could be identified.

7. 51mm Mortars were carried in the Warrior APC by rifle platoons. They could be used to fire smoke, illumination and High Explosive, over a range of up to 750 metres. Mortar Platoons were issued with the heavier 81mm weapon.

8. Anti-aircraft guns are still often called 'Flak' guns in military parlance, from the German military acronym for Flugzeug Abwehr Kanone.

9. The Forward Observation Officer, on attachment to the Battle Group from the Royal Artillery, carried a laser sight for directing artillery fire. This was a very accurate way of pinpointing a target.

Notes

Chapter 4 (pp 101–121)

1. During the Second World War the German Afrika Korps used 88mm Anti-Aircraft guns in a direct fire role as Anti-tank guns with devastating effect.
2. 7.62mm Machine-gun: one was mounted in the vehicle turret and each section carried at least one General Purpose Machine-gun in addition.
3. RPG7 was the standard Soviet hand-held Anti-tank rocket projector, similar to the Bazooka used by US Forces in the Second World War.

Chapter 5 (pp 122–134)

1. Vehicles in the Reconnaissance Platoon worked in pairs with one covering the other, therefore half the Platoon's vehicles each had an 'Alpha Call-sign' which was its counterpart with the same numerical Call-sign but with the suffix A (Alpha). Thus, vehicles 24 and 24A worked together and protected each other.
2. Schwarzkopf, General H. Norman, *It Doesn't Take a Hero*, Bantam, London, 1992.

Chapter 6 (pp 135–150)

1. Instead of cheering, Arabs (particularly women) 'Ululate'. They emit a shrill cry whilst moving their tongues rapidly from side to side.
2. Greeting is Scots dialect for weeping.

Appendix 1

AWARDS

MILITARY CROSS:

Major John Potter, The Royal Highland Fusiliers, attached
1 Royal Scots

Major Potter commanded B Company in 1 Royal Scots
Battle Group during the campaign. The Battle Group was
in contact with the enemy for the majority of the time and
B Company was left in front throughout. 1 Royal Scots
attacked three major objects and Major Potter's Company
was heavily involved. Wherever his Company was, his
vehicle could always be seen in the midst of the action. He
moved around constantly encouraging, leading, directing
and chastising, without regard for enemy fire or mines.

The first engagement for the Battle Group in Southern
Iraq began with tanks engaging an enemy artillery battery.
The night was pitch dark and rain obscured the image
intensification sights of the Warrior Armoured Personnel
Carrier. B Company moved forward either to force a
surrender or to complete the destruction of the enemy.

There were reports of mines in the area and the enemy had been engaging just to the North.

Major Potter co-ordinated a violent concentration of fire onto the objective and shortly after, the enemy began to surrender, Major Potter used headlight signals to encourage the others and soon the position was secured. Later, at another position, after a surrender, Major Potter gave clear instructions for the tending of enemy wounded and the burial of the dead. Under pressure to press on, he ensured that the worst of the wounded were carried forward with the Battle Group.

During the Battle Group attack on yet another position, Major Potter led his Company through a turmoil of dust, direct and indirect fire, to execute a classic rolling up operation. His awareness and steadiness helped him ease his company into position to exert an unsurvivable concentration of firepower. He executed the operation with ruthless efficiency and quickly redeployed to cover A Company's impending attack.

Following a further four attacks, and during a Battle Group replenishment, Major Potter's Company observed another enemy position which it immediately attacked and soon overcame. By this time Major Potter's Company had been in action or on the move for 48 hours and had had little sleep.

Major Potter's leadership was outstanding. He was cool under fire, calm in contact, resolute in danger and pursued the enemy with clinical ruthlessness. He was an example to all who knew him.

London Gazette 29 June 1991

MILITARY CROSS:

Captain (Acting Major) Norman Graeme Scott Soutar

Captain Soutar commanded A Company of 1 Royal Scots

Battle Group. Fifteen enemy positions were attacked by the Battle Group in all, and Captain Soutar's Company was involved in about half of these.

At the first position in Southern Iraq, Captain Soutar's Company was the right forward Company within the Battle Group. Shortly after midnight on a dark and very wet night, B Company assaulted a position, and whilst they reorganised, A Company was pushed forward with some tanks. Enemy guns were identified and, whilst the tanks destroyed them, Captain Soutar led a dismounted assault to clear enemy bunkers from around them. The area, according to a recently captured enemy prisoner of war, contained mines. The position was systematically cleared with grenades.

Later, at another position, Captain Soutar led his Company into a mounted assault. He chose to advance rapidly into his own artillery barrage in order to ensure the shock action of his attack. The enemy were at rifle point when they recovered. During reorganisation, his vehicles ran over a number of anti personnel mines and bomblets but Captain Soutar shepherded them to safety.

Thirty-two hours after the Battle Group left its original forming up point Captain Soutar's Company was still attacking. He was always forward and always ready to lead, whether mounted or on foot. He had trained his Company to be ruthless and they used their weapons to shocking effect and with chilling precision.

However, there were times when Captain Soutar personally put himself at risk in order to encourage the speedy surrender of enemy to allow the advance to continue.
He was a bold leader: decisive, brave, fit and not afraid of violence. He never placed himself at less risk than those he led and he offered a fine example of true leadership in battle.

London Gazette 29 June 1991

MILITARY MEDAL:

24780087 Private Thomas Robertson Gow

On 26 February 1991, 1 Royal Scots Battle Group was ordered to attack an enemy position in Southern Iraq as part of 4th Armoured Brigade's thrust East. B Company was tasked to assault a platoon objective which was well established and dug in. A preliminary phase of the operation had confirmed that there were T–55 tanks in the area. The position was subjected to an intense artillery bombardment which, combined with a strong wind, produced appalling visibility.

Five Platoon of B Company carried out a rolling assault on the northern end of the position whilst the remainder of the company provided fire support. As the attack proceeded it became apparent that at least one of the vehicles was too well dug in to be reached by Warrior Armoured Personnel Carriers.

Private Gow, who was acting as the section second in command, immediately appreciated the situation and saw that the momentum was being lost. On his own initiative, he ordered his fire team to cover him and crawled forward towards the vehicle. Despite the fact that mines and bomblets had already exploded on the objective, he got to a position within 20 metres of the enemy vehicle and destroyed it with his Close Assault Weapon and finished it off with a grenade. He then followed up by charging two bunkers, clearing them with grenades, without regard to the ammunition exploding around him. He captured three officers and four soldiers.

Private Gow had been in action for 24 hours and his section had already been involved in an assault before. The initiative, aggression and determination displayed by this brave man during this action exceeded that expected of his rank and experience.

London Gazette 29 June 1991

Appendix 1

MENTIONED IN DESPATCHES:

Lieutenant (now Captain) Angus Roderick McLeod, Commander Reconnaissance Platoon, Fire Support Company.

Sergeant Ian Copland, Reconnaissance Platoon, Fire Support Company.

Captain McLeod and Sgt Copland were Mentioned in Despatches for rescuing the crew of a vehicle which broke down under Iraqi fire in the opening stages of the assault on Objective TUNGSTEN. (see Chapter 5).

Private (now Lance Corporal) David Andrew Gibb, A Company

Lance Corporal Gibb was Mentioned in Despatches for his actions on 26 February 1991, when his Platoon Commander's vehicle shed a track on the approach to Objective BRASS. Gibb took control, prepared the vehicle for retrieval by the REME Light Aid Detachment and rounded up and searched a number of Iraqi prisoners, meanwhile keeping his Company Second in Command informed of the situation and his actions. (see Chapter 4).

G.O.C. 1 (BRITISH) DIVISION'S COMMENDATION:

Private Scott Gillies, Mortar Platoon, Fire Support Company.

Private Gillies, a medical orderly in the Mortar Platoon was on hand when a US Army 'Hummer' reconnaissance vehicle overturned and the two occupants were seriously injured. Gillies cleared a large bloodclot from the throat of the driver, who was unconscious, enabling him to breathe, administered Morphine and dressed the two US soldiers' wounds, and stayed with them until they could be evacuated by helicopter.

UNITED STATES ARMY COMMENDATION MEDAL:

Lance Corporal (now Corporal) Brian Edward Meechan, Regimental Medical Assistant, B Company.

Corporal Meechan tended the Iraqis who were wounded in B Company's assaults on Objectives BRONZE and BRASS. Despite their terrible wounds (see Chapters 3 & 4), he managed to stabilize them and prepare them for evacuation, and nearly all of the men he treated survived. The casualties were taken to a US military hospital, and the doctor who received them was so impressed with the way they had been prepared for evacuation that he recommended Corporal Meechan for this award.

MEMBER OF THE ORDER OF THE BRITISH EMPIRE (MILITARY DIVISION):

Captain Michael Low, Families Officer.
For his work as Families Officer during the Gulf conflict, Captain Low was appointed MBE in the New Year Honours list, 1992.

Appendix 2

ORGANIZATION AND ORDER OF BATTLE

1st Battalion The Royal Scots (The Royal Regiment), Order of Battle Operation GRANBY December, 1990–April, 1991

Battle Group Headquarters:

Commanding Officer	Lt. Colonel I. A. Johnstone OBE
2I/C	Major K. R. Gillies MBE
Adjutant	Captain G. E. Lowder
Regimental Sergeant Major	Warrant Officer 1 R. Frazer
Operations Officer	Captain N. Brownlie
Operations Training Warrant Officer	WO 2 Brown
Intelligence Officer	Captain D. J. P. Fulton
Regtl. Int. N.C.O.	Colour Sergeant Lusty
R.S.O.	Captain J. Springthorpe
R.S.W.O.	WO2 Harper
Watchkeeper/Training Officer	Captain S. F. M. Telfer
Watchkeeper	2 Lt Allsopp (Gren. Guards)
Watchkeeper	CSgt (Pipe Major) Cornwall
Liaison Officer	Lt A. D. Dockar
Liaison Officer	2Lt S. J. C. Henderson

Liaison Officer   2Lt. N. A. J. Moffat
Liaison Officer   2Lt. A. H. Palmer, A.A.C.

A COMPANY
Officer Commanding   Major N. G. S. Soutar MC
Coy 2IC   Capt. R. B. Bruce
2nd Captain   Lt C. T. O. Brannigan
CSM   WO 2 J. Flood
CQMS   Csgt J. Bain
1 Platoon Commander   Lt K. P. Douglas
2 Platoon Commander   2Lt H. G. Angus
3 Platoon Commander   Lt C. S. R. Dougan

B COMPANY
Officer Commanding   Major J. Potter RHF MC
Coy 2IC   Captain A. Alderson
2nd Captain   Captain T. A. Watters
CSM   WO2 Lumsden
CQMS   CSgt Mercer
4 Platoon Commander   Lt R. Dickson
5 Platoon Commander   Lt A. Stobie
6 Platoon Commander   2Lt R. Walker

FIRE SUPPORT COMPANY
Officer Commanding   Major B. C. Johnston, KOSB
                                      Captain J. I. Stephenson
(Major Johnston Casevac to UK as a result of a shooting accident on
Devil Dog Dragoon ranges.)
Coy 2I/C   Captain J. M. L. Gillespie-Payne
CSM   WO2 D. Dickson
CQMS   CSgt Johnstone
Mortar Platoon Commander   Captain A. D. Burnett
2I/C Mortar Pl   WO1 J. Gallagher
Reconnaissance Platoon
   Commander   Captain A. R. M. Mcleod
2I/C Recce Pl.   CSgt Spiers
Anti-Tank Platoon Commander   Lieutenant G. S. Richardson
2I/C Milan Pl   CSgt T. Butler
Mobile Main Section Cdr   Lt J. M. Donovan

REGIMENTAL AID POST
Regimental Medical Officer	Major R. Bissett RAMC
Regimental Medical Officer	Captain J. Timothy RAMC
Padre	Major S. Blakey
Ambulance Master	Captain P. Mehrlich Derr
Bandmaster	WOi Hodgetts

A2 ECHELON
O/C A2 / O/C HQ Coy.	Captain W. H. McGrath
2Ic HQ Coy.	Lt W. K. Smart WRAC
QM (T)	Major G. C. W. Waugh
RQMS	WO2 McConnell
CSM	WO2 Cochrane
CQMS	Sgt Finlay / CSgt Skirving
Master Chef	WO2 Evans ACC
EME	Captain M. Court REME
ASM	WO i Knighton REME
AQMS	WO2 Bradley ACC
QMS i APTC	Sgt Young APTC

Ai ECHELON
O/C / MTO	Captain D. L. Beveridge
RQMS (T)	WO2 Henderson
MTWO	WO2 Gilmour

Bi ECHELON
O/C / QM	Major J. Sands
Paymaster	Captain D. A. Restall

B2 ECHELON
Assistant Adjutant	Lt W. G. Sutherland
Chief Clerk	WO2 Livingstone

REAR PARTY
Officer Commanding	Major R. G. A. Blamire
Unit Families Officer	Captain M. C. Low, MBE

Appendix 3

GLOSSARY

Arms Plot – British Army parlance for the movement and rotation of units through the various depots and garrisons maintained in the UK and overseas.

A2 Echelon – The Battalion support line which also provided facilities for rest and recreation away from the Battalion's tactical area.

A Vehicles – Armoured vehicles, usually tracked.

BAOR – British Army of the Rhine.

BATUS – British Army Training Unit, Suffield (in Canada), a massive complex with tank and infantry ranges.

Bergen – Rucksack, copied from the type of pack carried by Norwegian soldiers and therefore named after Bergen in Norway.

BMP – Soviet-made armoured infantry fighting vehicle.

B Vehicles – Non-armoured, wheeled vehicles.

CBA – Combat Body Armour.

Challenger – The British Main Battle Tank in the Gulf.

CLAW – Close Light Assault Weapon, a rifle grenade which fitted over the muzzle of the SA80. It was already in service with the French armed forces, but had not been adopted by the British Army. It bridged the gap between the L2 hand grenade and the light mortar, and proved useful for destroying bunkers.

CVRT – Combat Vehicle Reconnaissance Tracked. The generic term for a series of vehicles including Scorpion, Striker, Samaritan, Sultan, and Scimitar.

Ferret – A wheeled armoured reconnaissance vehicle, a direct decendent of the Daimler armoured car in use during the Second World War.

FIBUA – Fighting in Built Up Areas.

FTX – Field Training Exercise.

FUP – Forming Up Position, an area in which units could reassemble after crossing the breach into Iraq.

FV432 – The armoured personnel carrier in general use before the introduction of 'Warrior'.

G Day – The day the ground war started, 24 February 1991.

GPMG – General Purpose Machine-Gun.

GRANBY – Computer-generated name for the deployment of British forces to the Gulf.

Jocks – The rank and file in a Scottish regiment.

LSW – Light Support Weapon, a heavier version of the SA80.

LAW80 – Light Anti-Tank Weapon: a hand-held wire-guided missile carried by each section when it deployed on the ground.

Milan – A wire-guided anti-tank missile.

MRE – Meal Ready to Eat – also popularly known as Meal Rejected by Ethiopia.

MTLB – Soviet made armoured personnel carrier.

NBC – Nuclear, Biological and Chemical.

OC – Officer Commanding, the term applied to Company and Platoon commanders, whereas the title Commanding Officer is only applied to the Battalion Commander.

O Group – Orders Group, when subordinate commanders are called in to receive orders.

ORBAT – Order of Battle: The structure of a military unit which could be altered to make it more suitable for a particular task.

PLCE – Personal Load Carrying Equipment.

RMA – Regimental Medical Assistant.

Roulement – The replacement of a unit in the field by another.

SA80 – The standard service firearm within the Battalion. It was capable of single shots or fully automatic fire, and was fitted with a magnified optical sight.

SATNAV – Satellite Navigation equipment which enabled vehicle commanders to establish their precise location and to find their way to any given map reference.

SITREP – Situation Report.

Staging Area – The area where units concentrated before moving off to cross the breach into Iraq.

Stand-To – A period when every soldier was at his post with his weapon ready, in case of attack, usually at dawn and dusk.

Start Line – A particular line, often a clearly defined terrain feature, which is used to co-ordinate the departure of a unit or units about to launch an attack.

Sultan – A light armoured command vehicle, one of the series of CVRT (Combat Vehicle Reconnaissance Tracked) currently in use.

Thermal Imaging – A sighting device which can pick up the 'heat signature' of a vehicle.

T-55 – Soviet-made battle tank.

Warrior – An armoured personnel carrier which carries a section of ten men, seven of whom can be deployed rapidly to carry out an infantry attack. The vehicle, which can be used to support the troops on the ground, is armed with an L21 30mm Rardon cannon, a Coaxial EX-34 7.62mm Hughes Helicopter Chain gun, smoke dischargers and 51mm Mortars.

Waypoint – A rendezvous point where the various units that are to go into an attack meet up before making their way to the Start Line.

BIBLIOGRAPHY

Published Sources:

al Khalil, S, *Republic of Fear*, Hutchinson Radius, London, 1991

Allen, C, *Thunder and Lightning*, HMSO, London, 1991

Beevor, A, *Inside the British Army*, Corgi Books, London, 1991

Benson, N, *Rats' Tales – The Staffordshire Regiment at War in the Gulf*, Brassey's, London, 1993

de la Billière, General Sir Peter, *Storm Command*, Harper Collins, London, 1992

Bryan, C D B, and Sygma Photographers, *In the Eye of Desert Storm*, Harry N Abrahams Inc, New York, 1991

Bulloch, J, and Morris, H, *Saddam's War*, Faber and Faber Ltd, London, 1991

Cordesman, A, *The Iran–Iraq War and Western Security 1984–87*, Jane's, London, 1987

Darwish, A, and Alexander, G, *Unholy Babylon*, Victor Gollancz, London, 1991

Bibliography

David, P, *Triumph in the Desert*, Century, London, 1991

Freedman, L, and Karsh, E, *The Gulf Conflict*, Faber and Faber, London, 1993

Gander, T J, *Nuclear, Biological & Chemical Warfare*, Ian Allan Ltd, London, 1987

Kay, Richard, *Desert Warrior*, Tenumbra Books, London, 1993

Moore, M, *Desert War*, Penguin Books, London, 1991

Pearce, N, *The Shield and the Sabre*, HMSO, London, 1992

Romano, S, *Desert Storm – The Gulf War in Colour*, Greenhill Books, London, 1991

Rottman, G, and Volstad, R, *Armies of the Gulf War*, Osprey Publishing Ltd, London, 1993

Salinger, P, *Secret Dossier – The Hidden Agenda Behind the Gulf War*, Penguin Books, London, 1991

Schwarzkopf, H Norman, *It Doesn't Take a Hero*, Bantam, London, 1992

Simpson, J, *From the House of War*, Arrow Books, London 1991

Stanwood, Dr F, Allen, P, and Peacock, L, *Gulf War*, William Heinemann Ltd, London, 1991

Warner, G, *Iraq and Syria 1941*, Davis Poynter, London, 1974

Watson, B, George, B, Tsouras, P, and Cyr, B, *Military Lessons of the Gulf War*, Greenhill Books, 1991

Witherow, J, and Sullivan, P, *The Sunday Times War in the Gulf – a Pictorial History*, Sidgwick & Jackson Ltd, London, 1991

Journals and newspapers:

The London Gazette
Soldier Magazine
The Thistle, Journal of the Royal Scots, (The Royal Regiment)
The Times

Bibliography

Unpublished Sources:

Private diary of Lieutenant (now Captain) Guy S. Richardson, Commander Anti-Tank Platoon

Private diary of Second Lieutenant (now Lieutenant) Roger M. Walker, Commander No 6 Platoon, B Company

Private diary of Corporal Derek Notman, No 6 Platoon, B Company

Private diary compiled by Major (now Lt. Colonel) John Potter MC, Commander, B Company

Lecture notes compiled by Lt. Colonel (now Brigadier) Iain A. Johnstone OBE, Commanding Officer

Summary of the Battalion's operations compiled by Captain (Retd) Neil Brownlie, Operations Officer

Sammy's War, by Corporal Brian Allen, an unpublished account of the work of the crew of 'Sammy the Samson', a REME recovery vehicle attached to the Royal Scots' Reconnaissance Platoon.

Recorded reminiscences of:

Battle Group Main:
Lieutenant Colonel (now Brigadier) Iain A. Johnstone OBE Commanding Officer
Major Kirk Gillies MBE – Battalion Second-in-Command
Captain (Retd) Neil Brownlie – Operations Officer
Captain Dermot Fulton – Intelligence Officer

A Company:
Captain Bob Bruce – Company Second-in-Command
Lieutenant (now Captain) Chris T. O. Brannigan – Warrior – Captain
Warrant Officer 2 James Flood – Company Sergeant Major
Lieutenant Kenny Douglas – Commander No 1 Platoon
Private (now Lance Corporal) John J. Drain – No 1 Platoon
Private Chris Owen – No 1 Platoon
Private Peter Pearson – No 1 Platoon

Corporal Billy Paul – Section Commander, No 2 Platton
Private Mervyn Dyer – No 2 Platoon
Private Vincent Stott – No 2 Platoon
Private (now Lance Corporal) David Gibb – No 2 Platoon
Lieutenant Colin Dougan – Commander No 3 Platoon

B Company:
Major (now Lt.Colonel) John Potter MC – Company Commander
Corporal Raymond 'Chats' Thompson – Company Signaller
Lance Corporal Brian E. Meechan – Company Medical Orderly
Lance Corporal Geoffrey I McDermid – No 4 Platoon
Lieutenant (now Captain) Alastair M. M. Stobie – Commander No 5 Platoon
Sergeant Tom Gorrian – Platoon Sergeant, No 5 Platoon
Private Tom Gow MM – No 5 Platoon
Private Kevin Newton – No 5 Platoon
Lieutenant Roger M Walker – Commander No 6 Platoon
Corporal Derek Notman – Section Commander, No 6 Platoon
Private Stuart McDonald – No 6 Platoon

Fire Support Company:
Major (retd) Bryan Johnston – Company Commander
Warrant Officer 2 Dave Dickson – Company Sergeant Major
Captain Angus McLeod – Commander Reconnaissance Platoon
Private Nick Williams – Reconnaissance Platoon
Lieutenant (now Captain) Guy S. Richardson – Commander Anti-Tank Platoon
Sergeant Peter Fagan – Mortar Fire Controller, Mortar Platoon
Private Scott Gillies – Mortar Platoon

HQ Company and Echelons:

Captain Bill McGrath – Company and A2 Echelon Commander

Lieutenant (now Captain) Wendy Smart – Second in Command

Major (Retd) G. C. W. 'Paddy' Waugh – Quartermaster (Technical)

Private Mark Morrice – A2 Echelon

Lieutenant (now Captain) Bill Sutherland – Assistant Adjutant, B2 Echelon

Author's note: Ranks cited with the reminiscences quoted in the text of this book are those held during the conflict.

INDEX

Index

Index

Index